HK+ National Strategies Research Project Agency, Center for International Area Studies, Hankuk University of Foreign Studies Seminar Series

# Border and Environment

## Supra-National Cooperation and Communication for Reaching Carbon Neutrality

This book was supported by the Ministry of Education of the Republic of Korea and National Research Foundation of Korea. (NRF-2020S1A6A3A04064633)

HK+ National Strategies Research Project Agency, Center for International Area Studies, Hankuk University of Foreign Studies Seminar Series

# Border and Environment

### Supra-National Cooperation and Communication for Reaching Carbon Neutrality

Edited by HK+ National Strategies Research Project Agency,
Center for International Area Studies,
Hankuk University of Foreign Studies

**Reece Jones** is a 2021 Guggenheim Fellow and a professor in and the chair of the Department of Geography and Environment at the University of Hawaii. He is the author of award-winning books, *Border Walls: security and the war on teerror in the United States, India, and Israel* (2012), *Violent Borders: Refugees and the Right to Move* (2016), and *White Borders: the history of race and immigration in the United States from Chinese exlusion to the border wall* (2021). He has also published dozens of research articles and newspaper columns on the roles that borders and immigration restrictions play. He is the editor in chief of the Journal Geopolitics and lives in Honolulu with his family.

**Wang, Hongxia** is a research professor and the director of Department of Population and Resources and Environmental Economics at the Institute of Economics, Shanghai Academy of Social Sciences. She received her Ph.D. in economics from Fudan University. She is a member of China Population Association, a council member of Shanghai Economics Association, a chief professor of Metropolis spatial Development Strategy & Policy Research

Innovation Think Tank, and a consultant for Shanghai municipal government, Zhejiang, Jiangsu, Anhui, Shandong, Hebei, Yunan, Guizhou, Qinghai, Xinjiang and Tibet. She has published 5 monographs and more than 30 academic papers in CSSCI journals such as "China Population Science", "Social Science", and "Shanghai Economic Research." She has also accomplished more than 10 projects funded by National Natural Science Foundation, National Social Science Foundation, Shanghai Social Science Foundation, and Shanghai Decision-making Consulting Projects Fund. Her research interest includes urban and regional development, industrial economy, energy economics, and environmental issues.

**Sergey Lukonin** is the head of Sector of Economy and Politics of China, Primakov National Research Institute of World Economy and International Relations, Russian Academy of Science. He received his Ph.D. in world economy from Institute of Far Eastern Studies, Russian Academy of Sciences. He was an associate professor at Plekhanov Russian University of Economics and a guest professor in School of Northeast Asia Studies at Shandong Univeristy. He serves as a member of expert council in Committe on Education and Science at the Russian Federal Assembly (State Duma). His area of research focuses upon security challenges and multilateral cooperation in the Asia-Pacific region, and Russian regional priorities and policy. He is the author, co-author and editor of over 230 academic papers published in Russia, the US, China Japan, the Republic of Korea, Singapore, Vietnam, India and European countries.

**Sebastian Maslow** is Senior Lecturer in International Relations at Sendai Shirayuri Women's College. He was an assistant professor in Center for East Asian Studies at Heidelberg University, an assistant professor in Graduate School of Law at Tohoku University, and a research fellow in Institute of Social Science at University of Tokyo. He is the co-editor of *Crisis Narratives, Institutional Change, and the Transformation of the Japanese State* (SUNY Press, 2021), and *Risk State: Japan's Foreign Policy in an Age of Uncertainty* (Routledge, 2015). He also serves as associate editor and book review editor of *Social Science Japan Journal*.

**Park, Kyoo-Hong,** is a professor in School of Civil and Environmental Engineering, Urban Design and Studies at Chung-Ang University. He received his Ph.D. in civil and environmental engineering from Northwestern University. He was the president of Korean Society of Water and Wastewater. He also served as the dean of the Graduate School of Construction Engineering at Chung-Ang University.

**Kang, Taek Goo,** is a senior research fellow in Korea Environment Institute and the director of the Center for Environmental Information of North Korea at Korea Environment Institute. He received his Ph.D. in international relations from Tsinghua University in China. He was the chairman of Sector on Energy and Environment at the Korean Association of International Studies and the editor of *Korean Political Science Review*. He also served as a member of

Education Committee at Ministry of Unification of Republic of Korea.

**Myeong, Soojeong,** is a senior research fellow at Korea Environment Institute. She received her Ph.D. in environmental and resource engineering from the State University of New York. She served as a review editor of Intergovernmental Panel on Climate Change (IPCC) AR6, a leader author of IPCC Special Report on Land (SRCCL), and a leader author of IPCC Special Report on Extreme Event and Adaptation (SREX). She was also the representative of Republic of Korea at Asia Pacific Network for Global Change Research (APN) Scientific Planning Group (SPG), serving as a co-chairs. She is the author of numerous studies on climate change and inter-Korean environmental cooperation.

**Jang, Won Seok,** is a researcher fellow at Korea Environment Institute. He received his Ph.D. in environmental and natural resources engineering from Purdue University. He was a graduate research assistant in the Department of Agriculture and Biological Engineering at Purdue University and a research fellow in the Sustainability Innovation Lab at Colorado (SILC) at the University of Colorado Boulder. He works now for the Division of Public Infrastructure Assessment in Environment Assessment Group at Korea Environment Institute.

This volume is the compilation of the papers submitted by scholars who presented at the international conference co-hosted by the Korea Environment Institute (KEI) and the HK+ National Strategies Research Project Agency in Center for International Area Studies at Hankuk University of Foreign Studies, titled "Border and Environment: Supra-National Cooperation and Communication for Reaching Carbon Neutrality," held in Seoul, South Korea in November 12, 2021. Amid the ongoing COVID-19 pandemic, the conference was devoted to the critical issue of addressing the climate change in the Korean Peninsula with the special focus on how to make possible cooperation between South Korea and North Korea beyond the inter-Korean border, or DMZ. The eight scholars, consisting of four Koreans, an American, a Chinese, a Russian, and a German residing in Japan, discussed various issues on border and environment as well as carbon neutrality. Subsequently, they all agreed to develop their ideas to take the form of research papers, which came to be published in this book.

HK+ National Strategies Research Project Agency was established in the

Center for International Area Studies(CIAS) at Hankuk University of Foreign Studies(HUFS) in 2020 with the approval of the National Research Foundation of Korea. HK+ CIAS has set the agenda as follows: "Searching for the Supra-National Cooperation and Communication: Identifying the Cultural Connections with the Northern Region and Building a Cultural Hub for the Creation of Unification Friendly Circumstances." Aimed at turning into a world-class think-tank dedicated to expertise on North Korea and the "Northern Region," defined as the Caucasus region, Central Asia, Far Eastern Europe, Mongolia, Northern-east China, and Russia. HK+ CIAS has the advantage of utilizing CIAS and HUFS's year long experience on area studies. HUFS is undoubtedly the top university in South Korea for language education and international studies. Since its establishment, HUFS has focused on teaching and training young generations. As one of the main research institution of HUFS, CIAS has been devoted to research and other academic activities with 14 area research institutes under its supervision.

The co-sponsor Korea Environment Institute (KEI) was originally founded in January 1993 as the Korea Environmental Technology Research Institute (KETRI) as the Korean government affiliated research agency on environmental issues. The organization was reformed and expanded in 1997 to become the Korea Environment Institute. KEI is dedicated to research and policy making regarding the environmental related issues, particularly such crucial topics as sustainable development and carbon neutrality.

Although the COVID-19 pandemic is still going on, the year of 2022 will become a turning point for the worldwide effort to stop climate change and achieve carbon neutrality. In addition, we look forward to seeing the strengthening of inter-Korean relations based on their mutual interest in carrying out cooperation to address climate change. We sincerely hope that this volume would contribute to that effort toward the net-zero and carbon neutral Korean Peninsula.

I would like to thank again every participant of the conference and the authors of the papers presented in this volume. I also hope that the discussion on the issues surrounding border and environment in the Korean Peninsula will lead to better cooperation and communication, eventually allowing us to reach carbon neutrality.

Kang, Jun Young
Head, HK+ National Strategies Research Project Agency &
Director, Center for International Area Studies,
Hankuk University of Foreign Studies

## Contents

Part 1 _____ Reece Jones

## The Border Wall on the Korean Peninsula in Global Context

Part 2 _____ Wang, Hongxia

## China's Low-Carbon Economy: Trends and Outlook

Part 3___ Sergey Lukonin

# Environmental Agenda and Practice of Using ESG Criteria in Russia

Part 4___ Sebastian Maslow

# From Green Growth to Green Diplomacy: Japanese Domestic and International Initiatives Towards a Carbon Neutral Society

# The Border Wall on the Korean Peninsula in Global Context

*"That is why the greatest danger of all is to allow new walls to divide us from one another."*

- Barack Obama, in a speech at the site of the Berlin Wall in 2008

## I. Introduction

There is a global trend toward hardened borders through the construction of walls and the use of high tech security infrastructure. This is evident from the United States to the European Union, across the Middle East and Asia (Jones 2012; Bissonette and Vallet 2020; Di Cintio 2012; Vallet 2014; Vallet and David 2012). In the United States, the 2016 presidential campaign revolved around Donald

Trump's pledge to build a border wall on the US-Mexico border, which he claimed would solve many of the United States' problems both economic and social. What was often lost was that at the time the US already had almost 700 miles of border walls which had been built in 2007-09 (Jones 2012).

The US was not alone in its turn to border walls in the first two decades of the twenty-first century. Elisabeth Vallet and Andreanne Bissonette have documented the increase in border walls around the world. They found that at the end of World War II there were about five border walls in the entire world (Vallet 2013; Bissonette and Vallet 2020). As late as the year 2000, there were only about fifteen (<figure 1>). However, in 2021, there are now seventy. To put it another way, over three quarters of the border walls in the world were built in the past twenty years. These walls have been built in places that might be predictable, like on the borders of countries like Israel, but also in a wide range of other locations that are not normally associated with border disputes. Even Norway built a border wall in the past decade.

With so many new walls going up, it is impossible to point to a single factor driving their construction but there are several similar trends that are described in this paper allowing the different walls to be grouped into a few categories (Till et al 2012; Rosière and Jones, 2011). These categories are the immigration walls, the anti-terrorism walls, and the territorial conflict walls.

The first section of this paper documents the shifting purpose of borders, and by extension border walls, through the history of humanity from ancient walls through the present day examples. The section frames this evolution in relation to the increasing power of the state in the global system. Over

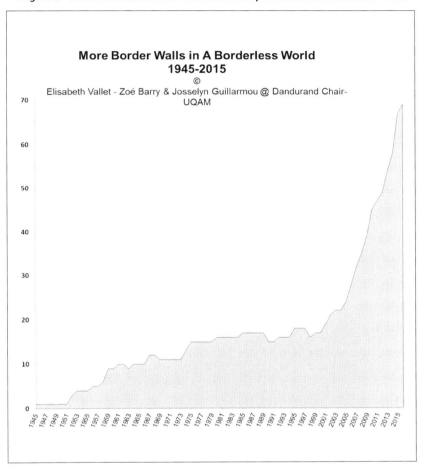

time, borders and border walls have transition from military defensive lines, to markers of state sovereignty, to finally the location to protect privileges by preventing the movement of the poor. This section of the paper considers historical examples of walls, such as the Great Walls of China and walls around medieval cities, in order to argue how they differ from the walls under construction around the world today. The second section of the paper analyzes the new border walls that have been built since World War II and categorizes them into different types of anti-terrorism, anti-immigration, and territorial conflict walls. The final section of the paper consider the wall on the Korean Peninsula and argues that it is one of the few remaining examples of a wall a type of wall from a previous purpose of a border and is best understood as a territorial conflict wall that is still serving as a military defensive line.

## II. The Shifting Purpose of Borders

James C. Scott has written extensively on the history of the state and the expansion of the state system around the world. In *The Art of Not Being Governed*, Scott summarizes the changing relationship between people and the state through different historical periods. He writes (2009, 324): "Simplifying greatly, we might identify four eras: 1) a stateless era (by far the longest), 2) an era of small-scale states encircled by vast and easily reached stateless peripheries, 3) a period in which such peripheries are shrunken and beleaguered by the expansion of state power, and finally, 4) an era in which virtually the entire global is 'administered space' and the periphery is not much more than a folkloric remnant."

Scott reminds us that the state is not a permanent political form, but one that emerged relatively recently in the history of the human presence on earth. For most of human history, there were not large scale political systems like the state that controlled vast swaths of territory. As Scott suggests, the state political form emerged in combination with sedentary agriculture. The earliest states developed as more workers were needed for large irrigation projects and as sedentary agriculture produced excess grain that could feed a non-agricultural population. These states were often based on slavery, capturing labor to work the fields, and established a hierarchical structure were an elite few controlled resources and wealth (Scott 2017).

It was not until the last two thousand years that these small, proto-states began to gain control over larger territories (Scott 2017). This process accelerated through new technologies that allowed states to monitor the activities of people far from the capital and eventually control large areas of the land through policing and bureaucracy. The early twentieth century was characterized by the rapid expansion state sovereignty into areas that had previously been outside the realm of control as road building, railroads, telephones, airplanes, and the internet allowed for the rapid deployment of state security forces and instant communication between the capital and farthest reaches of the state.

Scott (2009) suggests this process culminates with the post-World War II era in which the United Nation is established and control over most of the land in the world is settled. Today, the state is the dominant political structure and once a territory is assigned to a particular state, their control over that land is treated by other states as absolute and inviolable. The

United Nations plays a critical role in this process because it becomes the arbitrator or clearing house of global sovereignty claims. When a state joins the UN, they agree to recognize the territorial claims of all the other member states. Article 2 of the UN charter calls on all states to recognize the "sovereign equality of all its members" and "to refrain from international relations from the threat or use of force against the territorial integrity or political independence of any other state."[1] Consequently, in the UN era, most territorial claims have become more permanent as borders have remained in place. They are no longer simple the edges between two states, but also agreed upon by all of the other states in the global system.

## 1. Military Defensive Lines

My research on borders has contributed to this story by considering how the purpose of borders and walls has changed in each era. As early states were established, there was not a global system of mutual recognition of sovereignty (Johnson and Jones 2014; Jones 2016; Longo 2017). In the distant past, when states could expand out and take more land and resources, they did. They shrunk back when they were over extended. Consequently, they had edges, but they were not borders in the modern sense of the term. At the time, cartography was in its infancy and the ability to depict the world from above, a prerequisite for drawing borders on a map, was not yet possible (Blomley 2003; Harvey 1993; Harley 2002; Harley and Wood 1986). Consequently, the original purpose of borders were not agreed upon lines between different equal states but rather military defensive lines where one state defended its land, resources, and people from the threat of invasion by another state or non-state actors.

There are many examples of walls and fortifications from this era. The Great Walls of China are perhaps the most well-known (Lovell 2006). The first of these walls, built by Emperor Qin Shi Huang in 220 BC, were built because there was *not* a global system of territorial states and borders like we have today. They were not built on the borders of China that were depicted on a map because such a map did not exist and the concept of a territorial border was not yet imagined. Neither the Chinese emperors nor the nomads who raided their stores of rice recognized each other as the sovereign authority over a territory. When the nomads needed resources, they did not hesitate to raid agricultural towns for them. When the Chinese could, they organized armies to try to remove the nomads from the steppe. When that failed they built walls to try to prevent the raids on their resources.

Subsequent dynasties did build a series of discontinuous walls in various parts of Northern China over the next 1800 years. The Han (202 BC – 220 AD), the Jin Dynasty (256-420 AD), the Northern Qi (550-74 AD), the Sui (589-681 AD) and the Ming (1369-1644 AD) all built walls to protect their resources from the nomads in the north, mostly famously Genghis Khan. The Han, Jin, northern Qi, and Sui walls were constructed out of tamped earth and for the most part are gone due to weathering and damage by later generations. In some places a small line or mound is still visible in the landscape. In each case, the walls were a last, desperate attempt by emperors to protect their

**Great Walls of China**
- ·········· Pre-Qin Walls
- ·—·—· Qin Walls
- —— — Western Han Walls
- —·—— Jin Walls
- —— Ming Walls

Russia

Mongolia

Gobi Desert

Ordos Plateau

Beijing

China

Yellow River

Yellow Sea

Xianyang/Xi'an

rule. All were failures. Subsequent rulers often used different names for their projects, such as forts, barriers, frontiers, or fortifications, in order to avoid the negative stigma associated with *chang cheng* or 'long wall.'

In the late medieval period, the world continued to be characterized by overlapping and discontinuous areas of sovereignty. Even in densely populated Europe, the pattern of small states surrounded by vast partially or completely unknown areas continued through the 1500s. Big changes were coming in Europe, but they were not in place yet. Instead of the forty odd medium sized countries in Europe today, there were hundreds of tiny city states along with a few larger and discontinuous empires.

Most medieval cities had walls and fortifications to protect their people and resources in the event of an attack. All of these walls are early examples of political territoriality, the use of boundaries to define control over an area (Sack 1986). However, prior to the modern era, there was not a systematic use of bounded territories to signify political claims. The critical difference between modern sovereign states and these previous states is the mutual recognition of sovereignty—the right to establish and enforce laws—within bounded territories. Prior to the modern era, every ruler claimed absolute sovereignty for themselves, but did not recognize the sovereignty of other leaders. This resulted in many wars as each leader attempted to expand the land area under their control whenever it was possible militarily.

Walls and moats around medieval European cities served a similar purpose to the early walls in China (Jones 2016). They were defensive lines to prevent the invasion of another group. Because there was not a system of mutual recognition of sovereignty, every city was at risk of being attacked by its neighboring cities, by larger empires, and by mobile groups both small and large. The lords of the city made no pretense at being able to defend a large territory. Instead, the moat and wall around the city protected the most important resources. If a threat arrived, people could go inside the walls with stores of food, weapons, and wealth.

The walls around a medieval city in Europe are a good example of using boundaries to make an exclusive claim to power over a particular area. However, they also demonstrate that prior to the modern era, the extent of these claims to authority were limited by the lack of mapping and surveying technologies and of treaties between states. In medieval Europe, between the walls of one city and the walls of the next one thirty miles away was land with multiple and overlapping claims of authority. Neither city had the technology to map all of that land, which would allow them to agree on which parts belonged each city. There were not large centrally controlled states in Europe or anywhere in the world because the transportation and communication technologies necessary to administer them did not yet exist. Modern roads did not exist, phones, telegraphs, did not exist. The fastest news, tax collectors, or armies could travel was the speed of a horse or a ship. The farther you travelled away, the less control the city state had until there were areas of overlapping control or no control at all (Winichakul 1994).

## 2. Markers of Mutually Recognized Sovereignty

The purpose of borders started to shift with the development of the concept of mutual recognition of sovereignty. By the fifteenth and sixteenth centuries, states around the world had grown to the extent that they increasingly bumped up against each other in the pursuit of new land, resources, and people. Consequently, a new idea of mutually recognizing borders and territory emerged, and is often linked to the Treaties of Westphalia in 1648 that ended the Thirty Years War in Europe (Elden 2013). At that moment, advances in cartography had allowed the representation of the world from above and the new agreements between states included the idea to establish a line on the map and agree that each state would not cross that line and interfere in the territory of the state on the other side.

One of the first of these borders drawn on a map was the line between France and Spain which was established in 1659 in the Treaty of the Pyrenees (Sahlins 1991). Over the ensuing centuries, states around the world began the long process of establishing their borders with their neighbors. European states brought the system of border territories with them when they colonized much of the Americas, Africa, and Asia. After World War II, the second war of the twentieth century initiated by territorial expansion beyond agreed upon borders, the United Nations was established as a clearing house for borders and territorial claims. Once a country joins the UN, they pledge to respect both the borders and territories of all other member states, which has resulted in a stable period for borders around the world.

In the era of mutual recognition of sovereignty at borders, it no longer made sense to fortify borders with walls or other security measures. The treat of invasions across a border subsided and borders became the place where different political, cultural, and economic systems were bounded (Elden 2010, 2013; Walker 1993). For example, the United States is not worried that Canada is going to invade across the border. That is no longer the primary purpose the border served. For this reason, there were relatively few border walls built around the world during the era of mutual recognition of sovereignty. The ones that did exist are primarily on borders that are still functioning as the older purpose of military defensive lines, like the border in the Korean peninsula.

## 3. Barriers against the Movement of the Poor

The most recent shift in the purpose of borders has occurred over the past forty years (Brambilla 2015; Wilson and Donnan 2012). Over that period, the gap between the wealthiest and poorest states grew at the same time that population increased in many newly independent states. While in the nineteenth century, Europe was the region with a burgeoning population that was migrating around the world, in the late twentieth century, population growth was the largest in Asia and Africa. The result was more people attempting to migrate across borders.

The newest purpose of borders emerged in the era of globalization as borders became a line to prevent the movement of the poor and to protect the privileges that accrued in wealthy countries (Miller 2017; Pallister-Wilkins 2011; Parker et al 2009; Parker and Vaughan-Williams 2012; Walters 2015). While border walls were not necessary during the era of mutual recognition of sovereignty, walls became a powerful symbol for politicians in response to unauthorized movements of the poor (Brown 2010; Walia 2013, 2021). Consequently, the period of globalization, which was described as moving towards a borderless world, is also characterized by extensive bordering through the construction of walls and other security measures at borders (Andersson 2014; Ferdoush 2018; Johnson et al 2011; Slack et al 2018; Nail 2016).

Longo (2017) has suggested that the purpose of borders has begun to shift again to become a location where the states on either side work together to counter threats to their sovereign authority. This is evident in cross border cooperation against smuggling operations and the effort of the US and EU to push their borders out by paying neighboring countries to do border enforcement before migrants even reach their borders (Amilhat-Szary and Giraut 2015; Belcher et al 2015; Burridge et all 2017). The US-Mexico border is no longer a place where the two states are in conflict, but is the location they work together to thwart groups and individuals that do not respect their sovereign authority over the territory (Dear 2013).

## III. Border Walls Around the World

At general level, all of the new border walls built over the past twenty years can be understood in the context of preventing the movement of migrants at the edges of the state. However, with dozens of different examples, there are also differences in the local context in each instance. This paper argues there are three general categories for the justifications for existing border walls: terrorism-related walls, immigration-related walls, and walls related to territorial disputes.

The first round of walls built in the early 2000s were mostly justified on terrorism grounds. In the aftermath of the September 11 attack in the United States. The war on terror dominated global political discussions in the years that followed and early walls were framed in that context. The three walls I discuss in my book Border Walls (2012a), the US-Mexico wall built between 2007 and 2009, the Israeli wall in the West Bank built from 2002 –

2006 and the India wall on the border with Bangladesh were all represented as being primarily about terrorism prevention (see also Alatout 2009; Cohen 2006; Cons and Sanyal 2013; De León 2015; Jones 2012b; Rael 2017).

At first, even with the powerful language around terrorism prevention, many of these early walls were controversial. In the 1990s, the fall of the Berlin wall had been hailed as the symbolic fall of the entire communist system. The Berlin Wall had become a symbol of totalitarianism and its collapse symbolized the opening up of the world to capitalism and globalization. At the start of the twenty-first century, wall building had a stigma and it was not something that democratic states typically did. Consequently, the link to security and terrorism was crucial to making these early walls more palatable to the public in each country.

By the early 2010s, that justification was less salient and some scholars, including myself, through the era of wall construction was waning. Elisabeth Vallet, however, saw the emergence of a new narrative around immigration. She wrote (2013, 2), "What initially could be interpreted as a tightening of security spurred by 9/11 proved to be a ratchet effect produced by the reaction against fast-paced globalization, which had not been wholeheartedly embraced by many members of the international community." Similarly, Wendy Brown, who had argued that the walls were symptom of the decline of the state, revised her view in 2017 writing, "While the main thesis of *Walled States* may hold up, however, it is inadequate to recent developments in border fortifications, especially in the European Union" (Jones et al 2017).

The new border walls that have gone up around the world in the past decade, heavily concentrated at the edges of the European Union, are almost uniformly justified based on immigration. These have included walls built by Spain in their enclaves of Ceuta and Melilla in North Africa, by Greece on its border with Turkey, by Bulgaria on its border with Turkey, and by Hungary on its border with Serbia. In the last few years, many other countries have joined suit, including Lithuania, Poland, Slovenia, Bosnia, and even the United Kingdom, which supported new walls around the Channel tunnel near Calais, France. For all of these walls, the previous stigma that had been associated with wall building had completely disappeared and they were directly justified as walls against immigration.

While the more recent border walls have primarily been about terrorism and immigration, there are still several examples of a third type of border wall that harkens back to a previous purpose of borders: the territorial conflict wall. The few walls that were built in the mid-twentieth century tended to be at locations where the two states on either side did not agree on the border. These contested borders were often locations of lingering disputes from previous conflicts. Examples of this type of border wall are the line of control in Kashmir, where India and Pakistan continue to dispute control over the territory, the border between Cuba and the American military base at Guantanamo Bay, as well as the focus of the rest of this essay: the demilitarized zone on the Korean Peninsula.

## IV. The Barriers on the Korean Peninsula

The border wall on the Korean Peninsula stands out among the seventy other border walls around the world as one of the few examples of the older purpose of a wall, as a territorial marker between two states still in conflict over control of the region. This differs from North Korea's border with China, which also has a border wall, but is more squarely focused on preventing the movement of civilians (Lee and Lee 2021). While most countries around the world solidified their borders in the two decades after World War II by joining the United Nations and mutually recognizing the borders and territorial integrity of all the other member states around the world, the demilitarized zone on the Korean peninsula remains a stubborn reminder of the original purpose of borders as military defensive lines.

The demilitarized zone on the Korean Peninsula is 250 kilometers long and 4 kilometers wide. It was created in 1953 as part of the Korean Armistice Agreement between North Korea, China, and the United Nations Command, led by the United States military (Lee 2013). In addition to establishing the demilitarized zone, the agreement also included a cease fire and established guidelines for repatriating prisoners. The armistice agreement was meant to be temporary and to serve as an interim measure until a permanent peace agreement could be reached. However, almost seventy years later, that permanent peace agreement has remained elusive and the armistice terms and the demilitarized zone have remained in place since.

The DMZ roughly follows the path of the 38th parallel which had been the boundary between American-backed South Korean and Soviet Union-backed North Korean forces prior to the outbreak of hostilities in 1948 (Oberdorfer and Carlin 2013). Because a permanent peace agreement has not been reached, the two sides of the DMZ are among the most highly militarized borders in the world (Park 2019). The DMZ is also distinct from many other borders in that it is a zone, not a specific line. The 4 km buffer in between is a unique feature.

Consequently, the border walls that were built along the DMZ is among the older type of walls that mark an ongoing territorial dispute, rather than being primarily about terrorism or immigration. Both sides of the DMZ have concertina wire and fencing to prevent movement into the buffer zone between the countries. The DMZ itself has relatively little human presence, although there are landmines in section of it (Kuhn 2019). There are also a few efforts to create cross border connections, such as the Kaesong Industrial Complex in North Kirea (Doucette and Lee 2015).

Like many border walls around the world, the border barrier on the Korean Peninsula has been mythologized and turned into a symbol, particularly in the north. In 1990, Democratic People's Republic of Korea president Kim Il-Sung gave a speech calling the border wall on the Korean peninsula a "barrier of national division." In the speech, he claimed the wall was made of concrete and was five to eight meters high and nineteen meters. None of those claims are true, but nevertheless, KCNA, North Korean state media, has mentioned this imagery of a concrete wall over one hundred and fifty times in the years since (Herskovitz 2009).

Consequently, even though the Korean border wall is of an older and unusual type compared to other more recent examples, it still serves a powerful symbol role. The metaphor of a wall enclosing the state territory and dividing one side from the other is often more important than the physical characteristics of the wall itself.


## V. Conclusion

There is little doubt that border walls transform any landscape in which they are built. Border walls impact migration patterns, often sending people on the move to more dangerous places to cross. They also impact the environment by disrupting water flows after rain events and the paths of rivers and streams. In many locations, the walls cut off traditional animal migration routes, splitting traditional ranges in half.

Nevertheless, most scholars of border walls are in agreement that the most powerful role border walls play in the contemporary world is a symbolic one. The military role of border walls is obsolete. Tanks can smash through them and missiles and airplanes flight right over. Border walls are not very effective against the movement of migrants either. If they are not constantly watched, a wall is easily breached with a simple ladder, as the hundreds of ladders found along the US-Mexico border every year attest. Most border walls do not extend for the full length of the border and there are ways to go around them, but often in more dangerous locations like the deserts of the

US Southwest that result in more deaths. Border walls are also easy to tunnel underneath. The US Border Patrol has found over two hundred and fifty tunnels at the US-Mexico border since the 1990s (Phillips 2019). North Korea built an extensive network of tunnels under the border barriers along the DMZ on the Korean Peninsula (Kim 2021).

Consequently, walls, in and of themselves, are ancient and outdated technologies that do not work to prevent movement across the border. Nevertheless, countries around the world continue to build more border walls, despite the huge expense and lack of effectiveness. The reason for this is often political. Despite not actually stopping movement, the construction of a wall is a powerful symbol of what a government intends for its policy to be at the border. The wall symbolizes action and brings that action into being in a visible, physical form. This is why the border wall became the defining idea of the 2016 US presidential campaign of Donald Trump and it is also why so many politicians are turning to border walls even as their effectiveness is questionable.

In the end, regardless of whether the wall is meant to symbolize the exclusion of terrorists or migrants or the territorial extent of the state, walls have become an increasingly popular symbol of nationalism and state sovereignty in the era of globalization.

# China's Low-Carbon Economy:
# Trends and Outlook

## I. Introduction

On September 22, 2020, China proposed at the United Nations General Assembly that China's carbon dioxide emissions should strive to reach a peak before 2030 and achieve "carbon neutrality" by 2060. In order to fulfill the above-mentioned commitments made to the international community, China put forward in the outline of the country's fourteenth five-year development plan to improve the dual control system of total energy consumption and intensity, and implement the control of carbon intensity and total carbon emissions as a supplementary system. It means that China will begin to enter a new stage of simultaneous development with carbon emission intensity and total control.

Based on the analysis of China's carbon emissions current situation and the objective background of China and the world's low-carbon transitional development, this paper will discuss China's low-carbon economic development trends and its prospects in the future years. There are three parts: first, the Current situations of China's $CO_2$ emissions; second, China's low carbon transition process; and the third is the part of trends and outlook of China's low carbon economic development.

## II. Current Situation of China's CO₂ Emissions

### 1. Current status of total carbon emissions

China is the largest one of carbon dioxide emitter in the world, facing

**\<Figure 1\> CO₂ emissions share 2020**

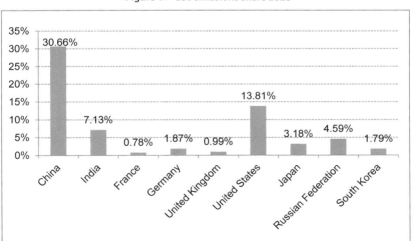

Source: bp's Statistical Review of World Energy 2021 (July 2021)

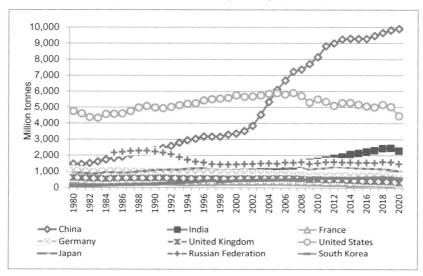

Source: bp's Statistical Review of World Energy 2021 (July 2021)

with greater pressure to reduce carbon emissions. China's total carbon dioxide emissions in 2020 were approximately 9.899 billion tonnes, accounting for 30.66% of global carbon dioxide emissions (BP, 2021). Compared with many countries in the world (see in <Figure 1> & <Figure 2>), China's total carbon dioxide emissions are large and account for a higher proportion of global carbon dioxide emissions. Therefore, for China there is a much greater pressure to control and reduce carbon dioxide emissions than other countries.

## 2. Per Capita CO₂ Emissions

China is one of the biggest countries in the world. According to the

<Figure 3> Per Capital CO₂ Emissions by Country(2020)

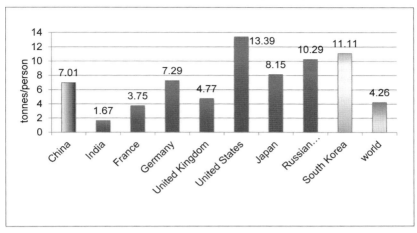

Source: CO₂ emissions data from the bp's Statistical Review of World Energy 2021 (July 2021) : Population Data taken
       from the official data released by each country

bulletin data issued by China's seventh national census in 2020, the total population of China is 1.4118 billion, accounting for approximately 18.61% of the world's total population.

In 2020, China's per capita carbon dioxide emission is 7.01 metric tons, higher than the global average of 4.26 metric tons of carbon dioxide emissions per capita. From a global perspective, China's per capita carbon dioxide emission level ranks 49th from the bottom among 209 countries and regions in the world, which is a low-to-medium level, and is lower than that of countries such as Germany, Japan, Russia, South Korea, and the United States (see <Figure 3>).

## 3. CO₂ Intensity

China's carbon dioxide emissions per unit GDP in 2020 is 6.7238 metric tons per 10,000 U.S. dollars, which is above the world average. By this indicator, there is a significant gap between China and developed countries such as the United States, Germany, the United Kingdom, France, Japan, and South Korea. (see <Figure 4>).

**<Figure 4> Carbon dioxide emissions per unit of GDP in Current USD(2020)**

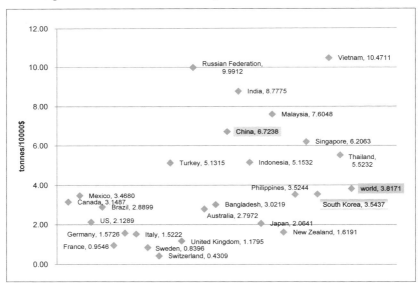

Source: CO₂ emissions data from the bp's Statistical Review of World Energy 2021 (July 2021) : GDP Data taken from World Bank national accounts data, and OECD National Accounts data files.

## 4. Current status of carbon emission structure

China's carbon dioxide emissions mainly come from the secondary industry sector. According to relevant data and research report data from China National Bureau of Statistics, at present, the share of carbon dioxide emissions in the secondary industry is still around 84% (see <Figure 5>).

<Figure 5> CO₂ emissions Industry Composition

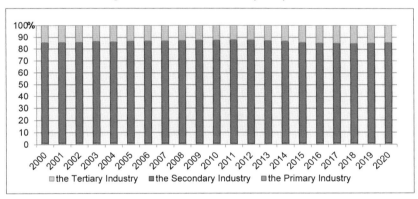

Source: Based on relevant data drawn from the National Bureau of Statistics project "Research on the Construction and Implementation Path of China's Horizontal Ecological Compensation Mechanism Index System."

## III. China's Low-carbon Transition and its Features

The original intention of the low-carbon economy is to fundamentally change the dependence of human production and life on petrochemical energy through technological and institutional innovation, reduce greenhouse gas emissions such as carbon dioxide, and achieve sustainable development characterized by low energy consumption, low emissions, and low pollution.

Back in 1997, the central government of China has proposed to transform the economic growth mode, changing the situation of high input, low output, high consumption, and low efficiency. Then in the 11th Five-Year Plan for National Economic and Social Development, for the first time, China central government clearly proposed to transform the economic development mode and advocate the development of a "low-carbon economy". Since 2009, it has accelerated the process of low-carbon economic transformation and introduced a series of policies to promote environmental protection and low-carbon economic development. Since 2011 China has incorporated reducing carbon intensity into the outline of the plans for national economic and social development as binding targets to fully respond to climate change. Since 2012, China has made unprecedented efforts to reduce carbon dioxide emissions, and made remarkable progress.

By the policy timeline, China's low-carbon transition process presents three development stages consistent with the implementation time of the above-mentioned policies. The extensive development stage before 1997; from 1997 to 2010, the stage of rapid growth of carbon emissions with the energy-saving and emission-reduction governance; and the stage of comprehensive carbon emission reduction since 2011 (see 〈Figure 6〉).

Studying China's low-carbon transition process, its characteristics can be found as the followings:

*First, the growth rate of total carbon dioxide emissions and the level of per*

<Figure 6> Trends of China energy Intensity, CO₂ Intensity and CO₂ emissions per capita:1980-2020

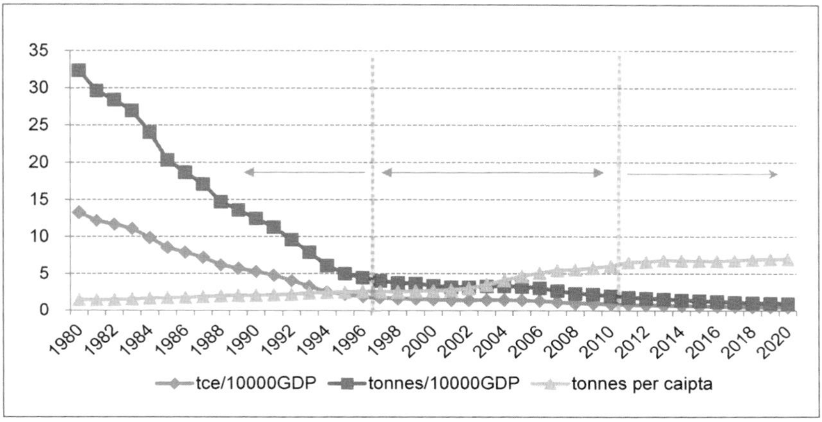

Source : GDP data and Energy Consumption data taken from CO₂ emissions data from China Statistical Yearbook 2020. China Energy Statistical Yearbook 2020. CO₂ emissions data from the bp's Statistical Review of World Energy 2021 (July 2021)

*capita carbon dioxide emissions have been significantly controlled in recent years.*

Although China's total carbon dioxide emissions are still at a relatively high level, the growth rate of total carbon dioxide emissions since 2009 has been significantly controlled. During the period 2009-2019, the average annual growth rate of China's carbon dioxide emissions was 2.43%, which was slightly higher than the world average and lower than that of some countries such as India during the same period.(see ⟨Figure 7⟩) Since 2013, China's per capita carbon dioxide emission level has been effectively controlled and basically maintained at the level of 6.79-7 tonnes/person (see ⟨Figure 8⟩). Especially since 2018, the annual growth rate of per capita carbon dioxide emissions has shown a clear downward trend. (see ⟨Figure 9⟩).

<Figure 7> CO₂ Emissions Growth rate per annum(2009-2019)

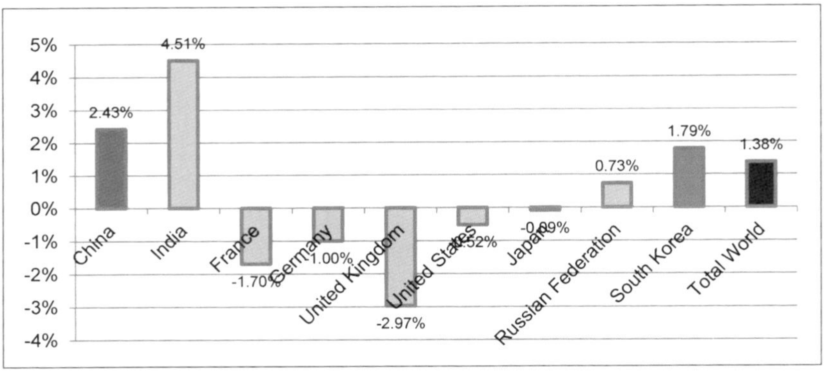

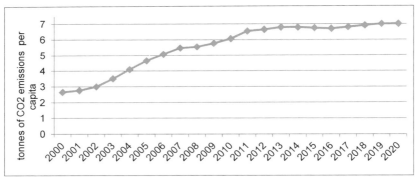

Source: CO₂ emissions data from the bp's Statistical Review of World Energy 2021 (July 2021)

<Figure 8> CO₂ emissions per capita (2000-2020)

Source: CO₂ emissions data from the bp's Statistical Review of World Energy 2021 (July 2021) : Population Data taken from National Bureau of Statistics of China.

*Second, China's carbon emission intensity has declined faster than the world average since 2004.*

The State Council Information Office of the People's Republic of China has just released the report on China's policies and actions to climate

Source: CO₂ emissions data from the bp's Statistical Review of World Energy 2021 (July 2021) : Population Data taken from National Bureau of Statistics of China.

change. According to the report, China's carbon intensity has decreased significantly. China's carbon intensity in 2020 was 18.8 percent lower than that in 2015, and 48.4 percent less than that in 2005, which means that China had more than fulfilled its commitment to the international community.

〈Figure 10〉 is China's carbon intensity growth trends from 1991 till now. It shows clearly that since 2004 China's carbon emission intensity has declined faster than the world average. It can be found that China has reversed the rapid growth of its carbon dioxide emissions since 2013.

*Thirdly, China's energy consumption structure has been rapidly optimized since 2011 but is still dominated by fossil energy.*

The proportion of China's fossil energy consumption has been declining since 2011, and the proportion of coal in total energy consumption

<Figure 10> Annual Growth Rate of CO₂ emissions Intensity Trends(1991-2018)

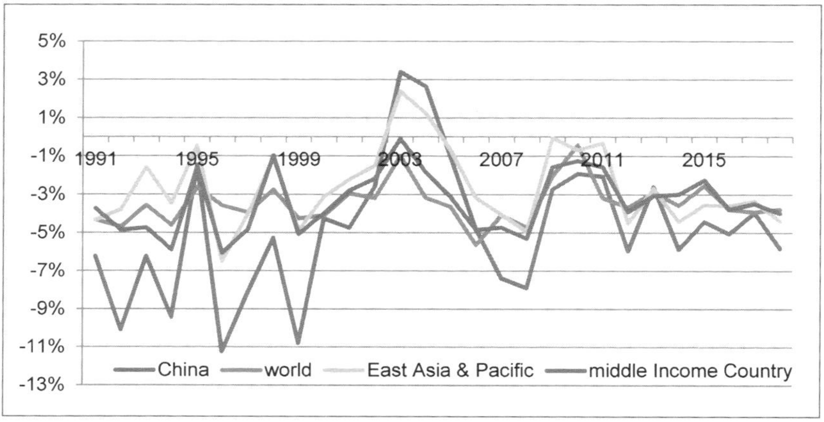

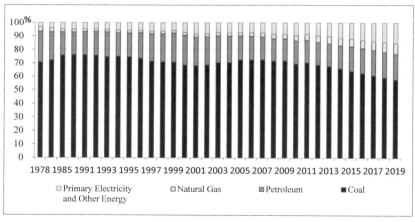

Source : Calculated with CO₂ emissions intensity data from World Development Indicators, Last Updated Date, World Bank (28 October 2021)

<Figure 11> Proportion to Total Energy Consumption(China)

Source: China Statistical Yearbook (2020)

has dropped significantly: At the end of 2019, China's coal consumption accounted for 57.7% of total energy consumption, a decrease of 12.5 percentage points compared to 2011. In recent years, the proportion of natural gas and primary energy consumption has continued to increase, reaching 23.4% at the end of 2019, an increase of 10.4 percentage points from this value in 2011. (see ⟨Figure 11⟩)

Overall, the proportion of fossil energy such as coal and oil in China's energy consumption is still as high as 76.6%. From the perspective of energy consumption in China's electricity production, coal-based thermal power generation provides 64.7% of the current electricity energy. (see ⟨Figure 12⟩). It can be concluded that China's current energy consumption structure is still dominated by fossil energy, and there is a lot of room for further optimization of the energy structure to reduce carbon emissions.

<Figure 12> 2019 Power Generation by Source

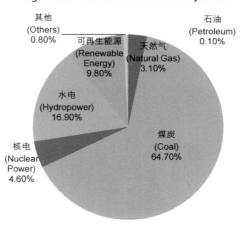

Source: China Statistical Yearbook (2020)

*Finally, Industrial structure adjustment, energy consumption structure optimization, and decline in energy intensity are all important factors improving China's low-carbon process.*

From the perspective of China's carbon emissions structure, the secondary industry sector is the main source of carbon emissions. And from the perspective of the energy composition of China's carbon emissions, carbon dioxide emissions from direct and indirect coal consumption are the main source of carbon emissions.

Through in-depth analysis of China's carbon emissions and the transformation of China's industrial structure, there have been studies that have found that the moderate control of China's total carbon emissions since 2011 is clearly related to the transformation of China's industrial structure since 2011 and the decline in the share of coal in energy consumption (Guan et al., 2018). The decline growth of $CO_2$ emissions is largely associated with changes in industrial structure and a decline in the share of coal used for energy.

From ⟨Figure 6⟩, which shows the changes in energy intensity and carbon intensity since 1980, it can be made a conclusion that the trend of energy intensity is basically synchronized with the trend of carbon intensity. Many studies have shown that decreasing energy intensity (energy per unit gross domestic product) and emissions intensity (emissions per unit energy) also contributed to the $CO_2$ emissions decline.

In fact, energy technology innovation and the promotion and application of new energy saving and environmental protection technologies have improved the technical level and efficiency of carbon emission factors, such as promoting complete combustion and improving thermal energy efficiency. These technological innovations have substantially promoted carbon reduction in recent years.

In addition, researches on the relationship between carbon emissions and economic growth also found that the slowdown in China's economic growth since 2011 has also reduced the growth of carbon emissions to a certain extent and promoted the process of carbon emission reduction(Wang et al., 2010).

## IV. Trends and Prospects of China's Low-carbon Economy

China has clearly stated in the outline of the fourteenth five-year development plan that it must implement a system which will focus on carbon intensity control and supplement total carbon emission control, and vigorously promote green and low-carbon development. China's carbon emission process is entering a new phase in which a low-carbon economy will lead smart carbon emission governance.

Under the background of China's low-carbon economic policy and the development status of low-carbon economy, China's low-carbon economy is showing the following development trends:

*First, it will be a low-carbon economy based on the optimization and adjustment of the national economic structure and industrial structure.*

In the framework of the influence of national economic structure and industrial structure on carbon emissions, China's low-carbon economy is going along the following three ways:

Ⅰ. National economic development moves to a Low-carbon development of mode.

Taking the reduction of energy consumption and carbon dioxide emissions per unit of GDP as indicator constraints, China seeks to promote the transformation of economic development mode to low-carbon and green, and realize low-carbon development.

Ⅱ. Optimizing and adjusting industrial structure to promote low-carbon development.

It is important to promote the optimization of the industrial structure, maintain a reasonable proportion of the industrial structure of the national economy, and achieve low-carbon development.

Since 2015, China's national economy has been an economy mainly featured by the tertiary industry. The tertiary industry's contribution to GDP has exceeded 55% since 2015, and the secondary industry's contribution to GDP has dropped to below 40% since 2015 (see 〈Figure 13〉). At present, China's secondary industry and tertiary industry respectively account for 37.8% and 54.5% of the national economy.

By comparing 〈Figure 5〉 with 〈Figure 13〉, it can be seen that China's GDP's three industrial structural adjustments seem to have not been synchronized with the structural changes in carbon emissions since 2015. It's secondary industry sector still accounts for a high proportion of carbon

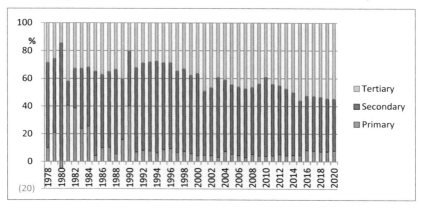

**<Figure 13> Share of the Contributions of the Three Strata of Industry**

Source: China Statistical Yearbook 2020, Statistical Communiqué of the People's Republic of China on the 2020 National Economic and Social Development, National Bureau of Statistics of China (28 February 2021).

emissions. Based on this fact, it can be inferred that under the current development background and trends, it may be more difficult to achieve low-carbon development by deeply adjusting and optimizing the industrial structure. How to maintain a reasonable proportion of the industrial structure of the national economy, and promote the adjustment and optimization of the industrial structure of the national economy, guided by the goal of carbon emission reduction, may be a more realistic path for a low-carbon economy.

Ⅲ. Controlling carbon emissions by watching on the sectors that are the main direct sources of carbon emissions, and vigorously promoting low-carbon development in the industrial sector.

In temrs of China's current main sources of carbon emissions, carbon

<Figure 14> Total Energy Consumption by Sector

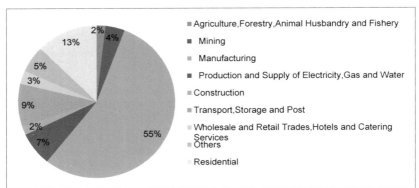

Source: China Energy Statistical Yearbook (2020)

emissions from the production sectors of the national economy, especially the industrial sectors of the secondary industry, are the main force. From the perspective of the sectoral composition of energy consumption, the manufacturing sector accounts for more than 55% of energy consumption and is the main sector of energy consumption (〈Figure 14〉).

Although there is a certain rigid relationship between China's energy production structure and energy consumption demand, adjusting and optimizing the energy structure is an inevitable solution to carbon emission reduction, and it is also the only choice that has to be made under actual technological innovation and economic constraints.

Under the current background of China's economic transformation, starting from the main sector of energy consumption and carbon emissions, the industrial sector, promoting energy conservation and emission reduction through energy structure optimization and energy efficiency improvement will be at least the main task and main contents of China's carbon emission reduction in the near future. Given that the decline in the energy intensity of the production sector is the most important factor in restraining the growth of $CO_2$ emissions, reducing the energy intensity of the production sector is a key measure to achieve $CO_2$ emissions reduction(Wang et al., 2010: Liu, 2012).

<Table 1> Proposition to Total Energy Consumption in Manufacturing Industry by Sector

| sector | percentage(%) |
|---|---|
| Smelting and Pressing of Ferrous Metals | 24.36 |
| Manufacture of Raw Chemical Materials and Chemical Products | 19.85 |
| Manufacture of Non-metallic Mineral Products | 12.42 |
| Processing of Petroleum, Coal and Other Fuels | 12.13 |
| Smelting and Pressing of Non-ferrous Metals | 9.10 |
| Manufacture of Textile | 2.76 |
| Manufacture of Metal Products | 2.44 |
| Manufacture of Computers, Communication and Other Electronic Equipment | 1.87 |
| Manufacture of Rubber and Plastics Products | 1.81 |
| Processing of Food from Agricultural Products | 1.54 |
| Manufacture of Paper and Paper Products | 1.43 |
| Manufacture of Automobiles | 1.36 |
| Manufacture of General Purpose Machinery | 1.35 |
| Manufacture of Electrical Machinery and Apparatus | 1.06 |
| Manufacture of Chemical Fibers | 0.90 |
| Manufacture of Medicines | 0.81 |
| Manufacture of Foods | 0.76 |
| Manufacture of Special Purpose Machinery | 0.70 |
| Other Manufacture | 0.67 |
| Manufacture of Liquor, Beverages and Refined Tea | 0.48 |

| sector | percentage(%) |
|---|---|
| Processing of Timber, Manufacture of Wood, Bamboo, Rattan, Palm, and Straw Products | 0.39 |
| Manufacture of Textile, Wearing Apparel and Accessories | 0.34 |
| Manufacture of Railway, Ship, Aerospace and Other Transport Equipments | 0.32 |
| Utilization of Waste Resources | 0.24 |
| Manufacture of Leather, Fur, Feather and Related Products and Footwear | 0.20 |
| Printing and Reproduction of Recording Media | 0.19 |
| Manufacture of Articles for Culture, Education, Arts and Crafts, Sport and Entertainment Activities | 0.18 |
| Manufacture of Furniture | 0.14 |
| Manufacture of Measuring Instruments and Machinery | 0.09 |
| Manufacture of Tobacco | 0.07 |
| Repair Service of Metal Products, Machinery and Equipment | 0.03 |
| Total | 100.00 |

Source: China Energy Statistical Yearbook (2020)

From the perspective of current energy consumption and carbon dioxide emissions subdivided industry sectors(see 〈Table 1〉), ferrous metal smelting, chemical manufacturing, non-metallic minerals manufacturing, petroleum and coal and its fuel processing, and non-ferrous metal smelting will be the most important sub-sectors affecting carbon emission reduction. It is foreseeable that in the next few years, these sub-sectors will face significant pressure on carbon emission reduction.

*Second, Energy structure optimization and low-carbon economic development based on energy consumption and use are needed.*

Controlling carbon emissions from the source of carbon emissions is the final way to achieve low-carbon economic development. The source of carbon emissions can be traced along the source of energy use and its technology. Therefore, to control carbon emissions in the field of energy use, carbon emissions can be reduced by optimizing the energy structure. While in the field of the technological roots of carbon emissions, the use of clean energy and technological innovation of carbon emissions can be used to control and reduce carbon emissions and promote the development of a low-carbon economy.

On October 24, 2021, the Central Committee of the Communist Party of China and the State Council of China issued the "Opinions on the Complete, Accurate and Comprehensive Implementation of the New Development Concept to Do a Good Job in Carbon Peak and Carbon Neutrality". On October 26, 2021, the State Council of China issued the "Notice on the Action Plan for Carbon Peaking by 2030". It proposes that, by 2025, carbon emissions per unit of GDP will be reduced by 18% compared to 2020, and the proportion of non-fossil energy consumption will reach about 20%; in 2030, carbon emissions per unit of GDP will be reduced by 65% compared with 2005, and the proportion of non-fossil energy consumption will reach about 25%; and the proportion of fossil energy consumption will reach about 80%. According to the plan of "carbon peak and carbon neutral" plan, by 2025 and 2030, China's non-fossil energy consumption proportion will strive to reach 20% and 25%, which are 4.6 and 9.6 percentage points higher than the proportion in 2020. In 2060, China's non-fossil energy consumption will reach 80%. To achieve this goal, China's non-fossil energy consumption ratio will reach an average annual growth rate of 1pct from 2025 to 2030, and an average annual growth rate of 1.83pct from 2030 to 2060.

China is further increasing energy structure adjustment and energy conservation and efficiency improvement. In 2020, the proportion of coal in energy consumption in China has dropped to about 56.8%, and the proportion of non-fossil energy in energy consumption has reached 15.9%. At the same time, China's energy-saving transformation is also accelerating. The coal consumption of coal-fired power plants continues to decline, and the energy consumption intensity has dropped by 28.7% from 2011 to 2020.

Although the current clean energy utilization technologies and carbon emission reduction technologies commonly used in China's industrial sectors have affected the carbon emission reduction process to a certain extent, the energy utilization efficiency and carbon emission technologies of China's industrial sectors are improving significantly, and energy technology innovation is accelerating .

China's new energy conservation, environmental protection and other strategic emerging industries are growing rapidly and will gradually become pillar industries. At present, the scale of production and sales of new energy vehicles ranks first in the world, and the wind power and photovoltaic power generation equipment manufacturing industry is forming the world's most complete industrial chain. In the future, in order to achieve the goal of "carbon peak and carbon neutrality", China's energy structure adjustment will be further strengthened.

The energy used by mankind is developing in the direction of high-carbon to low-carbon, low-efficiency to high-efficiency, unclean to clean, and from unsustainable to sustainable. Low-carbon economy and carbon emission reduction, in the final analysis, are actually energy efficiency and clean energy issues. The safe, clean, low-carbon and efficient transformation of China's energy system will be further strengthened, and the smart energy industry is expected to become an important growth point for the low-carbon economy.

*The third, also the last one, is to comprehensively promote green and low-carbon development, establish a carbon emission reduction ecosystem for production and life, and set up a low-carbon economy systematically.*

Low-carbon economy is a way of production and way of life. Under the UN SDG action framework, advocating the concept of green sustainable development and building a carbon emission reduction and low-carbon ecosystem for production and living are the fundamental guarantee for the ultimate realization of low-carbon development.

**<Table 2> Key areas of China's comprehensive low-carbon economy**

| Structures of a green and low-carbon circular development economic system | Main contents | Key Areas |
|---|---|---|
| Production system | Industrial green upgrading | Steel, petrochemical, chemical, non-ferrous, building materials, textile, paper, leather and other industries |
| | | Green Manufacturing System |

| Structures of a green and low-carbon circular development economic system | Main contents | Key Areas |
|---|---|---|
| Production system | Agricultural green development | Ecological planting, ecological breeding, green food, organic agricultural products |
| | | Ecological circular agriculture, forestry circular economy |
| | Green development of the service industry | Business and trading |
| | | Green Transformation of Information Service Industry Information Service Industry |
| | | Exhibition industry (hotel, catering) |
| | Green environmental protection industry | Environmental hosting service |
| | | Competitive business of energy conservation and environmental protection in the fields of petroleum, chemical industry, electric power, natural gas, etc., energy custody service |
| | SDG transformation of industrial parks | Industrial Cycle Coupling |
| | Green supply chain | supply chain |
| Circulation system | Green Logistics | Green low-carbon transportation |
| | Recycling of renewable resources | Recycling of renewable resources |
| | Green trade | Green product trade |
| | | Green Standard International Cooperation |
| | | energy conservation, environmental protection, clean energy and other fields |
| Consumption system | Green product | Green living consumption |
| | | Green power consumption |
| | Green and low-carbon life | Green and low-carbon lifestyle |
| Green infrastructure system | green and low-carbon transition of Energy system | Renewable energy use |
| | | large-capacity energy storage technology |
| | | Rural clean energy supply |
| | | Clean and efficient development, conversion and utilization of burning coal |
| | | Energy transmission and distribution efficiency |

| Structures of a green and low-carbon circular development economic system | Main contents | Key Areas |
|---|---|---|
| Green infrastructure system | Urban environmental infrastructure | Urban environmental infrastructure upgrading |
| | Transport infrastructure | Green Transport infrastructure |
| Green Technology Innovation System | Green and low-carbon technology R&D | Low-carbon technology support |
| | Green technology application | Green technology application promotion |

In February 2021, the State Council of China issued the "Guiding Opinions on Accelerating the Establishment and Improvement of a Green and Low-Carbon Circular Development Economic System", which advocates the concept of green sustainable development, and proposes to "implement green planning, green design, green investment, green construction, green production, green circulation, green life, and green consumption in an all-round and whole process", and coordinate the establishment of a green and low-carbon circular development economic system. In the context of present policy background and the current situation, China will comprehensively carry out carbon emission reduction in multi-dimensional key areas such as production, distribution, consumption, infrastructure, and technological innovation (see 〈Table 2〉), and promote a comprehensive low-carbon transformation of national economic and social development.

## Part 3

Sergey Lukonin

# Environmental Agenda and Practice of Using ESG Criteria in Russia

## I. Introduction

Environmental agenda and the practice of using ESG criteria have been perceived as an important issue in Russia. This paper will examine the current trend in Russia with the analysis of international agreements that Russia has made, Russia's national legislations, obligations, and interim results as well as its implementation of ESG criteria.

## II. International agreements

Russia has joined almost all major international documents defining the global environmental agenda. Among them:

- United Nations Framework Convention on Climate Change of 1992
  – Russia ratified it in 1994;[1]
- Kyoto Protocol to the United Nations Framework Convention on
  Climate Change of 1997 – Russia ratified it in 2004;[2]
- The Paris Agreement of 2015 – Russia, like other participating
  countries, signed it in 2016 and ratified in 2019;[3]
- and the Declaration on forests and land use proposed at the 26th
  United Nations Climate Change Conference in November 2021.[4]

Russia also participates in a number of multilateral treaties and
agreements in the field of environmental protection within the framework
of the Shanghai Cooperation Organization, the Eurasian Economic Union
and the Commonwealth of Independent States. For example, within the
framework of the Eurasian Economic Union there is the Agreement on
the Transboundary movement of Hazardous Waste through the Customs
Territory of the Eurasian Economic Union,[5] etc. Within the Commonwealth
of Independent States – it is the Agreement on cooperation in the field of
environmental protection,[6] the Agreement on information cooperation in
the field of ecology and environmental protection,[7] etc.

There are also a number of bilateral agreements, for example:

- with South Korea – Agreement on the protection of migratory birds,
  as well as a framework Agreement on cooperation in the field of
  environmental protection;
- with China – Agreement on joint Protection of Forests from Fires,
  Agreement on Cooperation in the Joint Development of Forest

Resources, Agreement on Cooperation in the Field of Research and Use of the World Ocean;

- with Germany – a framework Agreement on cooperation in the field of environmental protection, as well as a Memorandum of Understanding on cooperation between the Committee of the Russian Federation for Geology and the Use of Subsurface Resources and the Federal Institute for Geological Sciences and Natural Resources of Germany;

- with the USA – framework Agreement on cooperation in the field of environmental protection and natural resources.[8]

Similar treaties, agreements, protocols and memoranda have been concluded between Russia and the United Kingdom, Belgium, Finland, Sweden and other countries.

On the basis of supranational organizations, within the framework of international agreements, Russia also participates in the implementation of international environmental projects, for example, in the program for the conservation of Arctic flora and fauna of the Arctic Council.

## III. National legislation

The basic Russian national document in the field of environmental protection is the Federal Law "On Environmental Protection".[9] Its main terms are further specified by federal laws "On the protection of atmospheric air";[10] "On production waste";[11] "On Environmental expertise";[12] "On specially protected natural territories",[13] etc.

In addition, Russia's strategy on the field of the environment is explained in Environmental Safety Strategy of the Russian Federation for the period up to 2025,[14] which involves the following tasks:

- reducing the level of air pollution;
- increasing the level of waste disposal;
- preventing water pollution and improving water quality in polluted facilities;
- introducing innovative environmental technologies in production;
- as well as preserving the biological diversity of terrestrial and marine ecosystems.

Recently on November 1st, 2021, the Russian government approved a Strategy for the socio-economic development of Russia with low greenhouse gas emissions until 2050.[15] The priority of that Strategy is to reduce the accumulated volume of net greenhouse gas emissions in the Russia during the period from 2021 to 2050 to lower values in comparison with the same indicators of the European Union. It is assumed that further implementation of the Strategy will allow achieving carbon neutrality by 2060, but a final plan of specific measures for the implementation of that Strategy is still being developed.

There are also several projects implementing in Russia now: the national project "Ecology"[16] and the part of it — two federal projects "Clean Air"[17] and "Best Available Technologies". The federal project was completed ahead of schedule on 31st of December 2020. Some activities were transferred to the federal projects "Clean Air" and "Volga Health Improvement."[18]

The national project "Ecology" is aimed at the effective management of production and consumption waste, the elimination of unauthorized landfills, reducing the level of pollutants into the atmosphere, improving the quality of drinking water, preserving the unique water systems of Lake Baikal and Lake Teletskoye, etc.

All subprojects are designed until 2024 and assumes total financing in the amount 4 trln RUB (about 50 bln USD).[19] In projects involved various ministries and departments, for example, the Ministry of Natural Resources, the Ministry of Industry and Trade, the Ministry of Construction, Russian State Atomic Energy Corporation Rosatom, etc.

In general, these projects provide for the reduction of greenhouse gas emissions, stimulate Russian business to introduce the best green technologies, and also develop regulation of emission quotas.

Considering the above, Russia officially supports the main global initiatives aimed at protecting the environment and is quite deeply integrated into the emerging global environmental legal regime.

A broad environmental protection regime and a body of laws and regulations have also been formed within Russia, which establish the main directions of the Russian environmental strategy, its specific goals and indicators, as well as responsibility for violations of Russian environmental legislation.

## IV. Obligations

Under the Kyoto Protocol, Russia has committed itself to reduce total annual greenhouse gas emissions in the period from 2008 to 2012 by an average of 5% compared to 1990 levels. According to the data of the Ministry of Economic Development of the Russian Federation from 1991 to 2015 Russia was the world leader in terms of reducing greenhouse gas emissions (〈Figure 1〉).[20]

In 2015, Russia's greenhouse gas emissions from all sources were 44% lower than in 1990 – this is one of the highest reduction rates in the world. Greenhouse gas emissions from the energy sector in 2015 were

<Figure 1> Annual CO₂ emissions in Russia, USA, China and EU in 1990-2020 (bln t)*

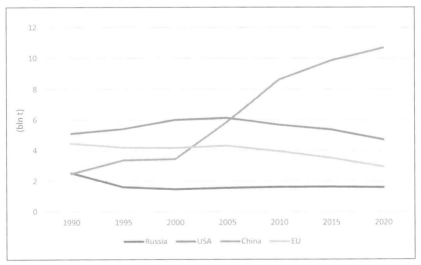

* Carbon dioxide (CO₂) emissions from the burning of fossil fuels for energy and cement production. Land use change is not included. Source: https://ourworldindata.org/co2/country/russia?country=~RUS

29% lower than in 1990; from fuel combustion decreased by 39%; from industrial processes — by 28%; from agricultural activities — by 60%.[21]

Within the framework of the Paris Agreement, Russia has set a goal for itself to reduce greenhouse gas emissions by 2030 to 70% relative to 1990 indicators, including taking into account the absorption capacity of forests.[22]

The structure of emissions by sector in Russia has remained relatively stable over the past decades. Most of the greenhouse gas emissions traditionally fall on the energy sector — its share in the total volume of emissions in 2018 was 78.9%, which is by 1.7 percentage points less than in 1990. The share of emissions from industry was 11.0% — by 2.1 percentage points higher than in 1990. And the share of emissions from agriculture was 5.7% — by 3.0 percentage points lower than in 1990.

In general, in 2018 the volume of greenhouse gas emissions from the Russian industrial sector decreased by 14.2% compared to 1990.[23] It means that at first sight Russia has exceeded its commitments under the Kyoto Protocol and, according to most indicators, successfully fulfills its obligations under the Paris Agreement.

## V. Interim results

During 1990–1998, there was a significant decrease in greenhouse gas emissions in Russia due to the general deterioration of the economic situation after the collapse of the USSR, namely, the degradation of industry and the disappearance of some of soviet industries.

In 1999–2008, during the period of economic recovery, which took place in both production and consumption, emissions showed steady growth, but the increase in emissions during this period was significantly lower than their reduction in the 1990s after USSR collapse. In 2009, there was a decline in emissions associated with the 2008 global economic crisis affecting the Russian Federation. In 2010–2012, during the post-crisis economic recovery, emissions began to increase again,[24] In 2013–2014, total greenhouse gas emissions decreased somewhat again due to the negative economic situation including associated with the Ukrainian crisis and the subsequent anti-Russian sanctions.[25]

In recent years the total greenhouse gas emissions increased slightly. But in 2019–2020 Russia has reduced greenhouse gas emissions by 4% – this is above the global average and slightly below the level of the G7 countries.

In general, in the period from 2000 by 2020 the Russian Federation reduced $CO_2$ emissions faster than many countries – by an average of 2.7% per year against 1.5% of the global average (〈Figure 2〉).[26]

However, the rate of reduction has decreased – if before the Paris Agreement in 2010–2015 they were 3.6% per year, then after it – an average of 1.9%.[27] This was partly due to the launch of the import substitution program – that is, the development of certain types of industries on the territory of Russia.

<Figure 2> Annual share of global $CO_2$ emissions by Russia, USA, China and EU*

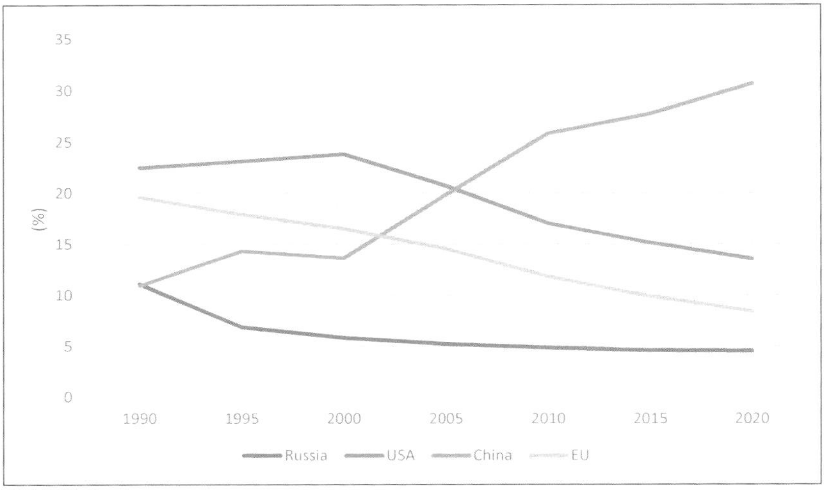

Source: https://ourworldindata.org/co2/country/russia?country=~RUS

## VI. General conclusions

On the one hand, Russia has made significant progress in reducing greenhouse gas emissions, has formed an environmentally friendly energy balance, dominated by natural gas, has joined to almost all international agreements aimed at preserving the environment, has developed and is implementing an ecology strategy, and also developed and implemented broad national environmental legislation.

On the other hand, Russia's environmental policy is still not active enough and is in the process of rethinking due to the global energy transition, primarily in the countries that are the main consumers of Russian energy resources.

Since the 1990s environmental policy has been perceived in Russia rather as a burden, and sometimes as a threat to economic development. This is most obviously shown in the National Security Strategy of the Russian Federation, where the development of "green technologies" is ranked among the main challenges and threats to the economic security of the country.[28] Primarily because that these technologies reduce the demand for raw materials exported by Russia.

Yes, Russia is a one of the world leaders in terms of reducing many types of pollution, as well as $CO_2$ emissions over the past three decades. However, this happened, rather, not because of the state environmental policy, but because of the USSR collapse: firstly, the territory of the country decreased, secondly, production chains were broken, and thirdly, some types of industry ceased to exist. All this has led to a reduction in harmful emissions, both statistically and in practice.

Russia's industrial potential has not yet recovered. Therefore, there is the statistical contradiction: even if Russia slightly increases the rate of greenhouse gas emissions in the coming years, statistically the general volume of greenhouse gas emissions will still be lower than in 1990 and Russia will still be able to fulfill its obligations under the Paris Agreement for example.

Of course, as stated above, some successes also were reached due to restructuring in the Russian electric power industry. A relatively favorable energy balance has been formed: with the dominance of natural gas (46%) and a high proportion of low-carbon nuclear (19%) and hydropower (18%).[29]

This energy balance is more preferable than in most developed countries, including Germany and the United States, which now consider themselves as leaders of low-carbon transformation, not to mention China and India, whose energy is traditionally based on coal.

Nevertheless, Russia lags significantly behind in terms of the carbon intensity of the economy from leading countries: firstly, because of the high share of heat generation (this is due to the harsh climate), and secondly, because of the low energy efficiency of the economy.

Some positive effect can be found in the transformation of the Russian economy in 1999-2007, when new, more high-tech and less harmful industries appeared. There was also a renewal of such industries as metallurgy and chemical industry, the development of nuclear and hydropower, the spread of modern gas electricity and heat generation.[30]

But today, the environmental situation in Russia is ambiguous. On the one hand, against the global background, Russia by some indicators remains a relatively environmentally prosperous country, for example, by the area of forests or by the structure of the balance of electricity production.

However, on the other hand, in a number of regions and cities, environmental problems reach a critical level. According to the Russian Federal Service for Supervision of Natural Resources, as of October 2021, Norilsk, Cherepovets and Novokuznetsk are recognized as the most polluting cities in Russia.[31] In May 2020, a diesel fuel spill occurred on the territory of one of the subsidiaries of the Russian company Norilsk Nickel. The total area of pollution, according to the Krasnoyarsk prosecutor's office, amounted to 180 thousand square meters.[32] This accident could become the largest known oil spill in the Russian Arctic. The largest such accident in the world is considered to be the catastrophe of the Exxon Valdez tanker in Alaska, during which, according to official data, about 36 thousand tons of oil leaked into the sea.[33]

Russia is a party of all major environmental agreements, including the Paris Agreement, and is developing cooperation on environmental issues with partners within the EAEU, BRICS, SCO, as well as with the countries of the European Union.

At the same time Russia is not trying to play a leading role in these processes and does not approach environmental issues as one of the real foreign policy priorities.

Passivity characterizes Russia's approach to the environmental and climate agenda both in relations with its BRICS and SCO partners and in relations with Western countries. Russia's chairmanship in BRICS and SCO in 2020 showed that Moscow does not consider ecological agenda as one of the priorities.

However, the situation is gradually changing and there is already an understanding in Russia that it is impossible to ignore the global trend of decarbonization, which directly affects Russian economic interests.

A decrease in demand for oil and gas will lead to a decrease in Russia's political and economic role in the world, since oil and gas remain the main Russian export positions. This is especially actual against the background of statements by the EU and China, the main importers of Russian energy carriers, about the creation of a green economy.

Russia relies on the development of nuclear (the possibility of recognizing the nuclear power industry as carbon neutral is currently being discussed), hydro- and hydrogen electric power, as well as on the expansion of the forest area. Currently, Russian Rosatom and Gazprom are studying various possibilities of exporting or producing green or blue hydrogen based on Russian gas to the EU.

The expansion of the area of Russian forests will increase their absorption capacity, and on that basis, it is possible to form some kind of "green" financial instruments and trading by emissions quotas.

There is little concrete information in this area yet, because there are many technical limitation. Russia is at the initial stage of forming its environmental, socio-economic policy.

In September 2021, the Russian Government began preparing a plan for adapting the Russian economy to the global energy transition. As part of the plan, special working groups were created under the leadership of vice premiers. Six ministries are also involved in the work: the Ministry of Economic Development, the Ministry of Industry and Trade, the Ministry of Energy, the Ministry of Natural Resources, the Ministry of Education and Science and the Ministry of Foreign Affairs.[34]

The Russian Government is also planning to launch a series of carbon neutrality experiments. In December 2021, a draft law on conducting the first experiment on the territory of the Sakhalin Region was submitted to the State Duma (Russian parliament) for consideration. It is assumed that carbon neutrality in this region will be achieved by 2025.[35]

The draft law establishes greenhouse gas emission quotas, introduces stricter and more mandatory reporting, and establishes penalties for violation of greenhouse gas emission quotas. The draft law also provides incentives for companies to achieve carbon neutrality: tax deductions and subsidies related to the reimbursement of production costs. In case of success, other regions may join the experiments.

## VII. ESG

ESG criteria are not widely used in Russia yet. Their implementation is only at the initial stage, and the legal environment is in the process of formation. Individual companies are trying to implement ESG practices, however, their number is small and until recently, the use of these criteria was more about image than efficiency. For example, according to a Deloitte CIS study conducted in 2021, the share of Russian banks applying any ESG practices in their activities is only about 10% of their total number in Russia.[36]

Most experts agree that there is no systematic approach to the implementation of ESG principles in banking practice yet. The Central Bank of Russia confirms that so far, the main focus of attention of banking sector regulators is not ESG practices in general, but proper assessment of financial risks.[37]

Any deals linked to ESG indicators are not very common, but there are examples – the interest rate on Russian bank "Sberbank" credit line for the Russian corporation "Sistema" for 10 bln RUB (about 130 mln US dollars) is tied to conditions such as the company's approval of environmental policy and the integration of ESG principles into the investment process and business model.[38] Currently, Citibank is working on a number of Russian deals containing ESG indicators.

In 2020, the Russian "Moscow Credit Bank" attracted a 20 mln US dollars loan tied to ESG indicators from German Landesbank Baden–Wuerttemberg.[39] In early 2021 Russian bank "Sovcombank" placed social Eurobonds for 300 mln euros also linked to ESG criteria.[40] Shares of five ESG mutual funds with assets of about 8 bln RUB (102 mln US dollars) are traded on the Russian capital market.[41] Russian companies "VEB", "Rosbank", "Russian Railways" and "GTLK", as well as the Moscow government have already announced their plans for green bonds. Russian company MTS plans to issue social bonds connected to ESG criteria in 2022.[42]

One of the Russian rating agencies evaluates Russian companies for the use of ESG practices and assigns a rating – now there are more than 150 such companies from 24 different industries.[43] Since February 2021, the Central Bank of Russia has started recruiting employees to a new division that will deal with sustainable development issues, including in accordance with ESG practices.[44]

In general, as of November 2021, the volume of issuance of bonds that take into account ESG criteria reached more than 125 bln RUB (about 1,6 bln US dollars), but 100 billion rubles fell on the securities of only one Russian company – "Russian Railways".[45]

At the same time, it is too early to talk about the sustainability of demand for ESG strategies. Risk and profitability remain the basis of decision-making for Russian companies. Many investors remain cautious, because bigger part of them traditionally associate ESG exclusively only with environmental initiatives, green startups, etc.

But Russian companies see for themselves new market niches opening up in connection with the "green" transformation of the world economy. For example, Russian company "Rusal" has offered a brand of the world's lowest-carbon aluminum.[46]

In general, Russian business began to actively show interest in the ESG criteria only in 2018, after the refusal of the Norwegian state Pension Fund to invest in Russian business due to poor ESG indicators. This pushed Russian business to increase investments in environmental and social projects. Russian companies are still lagging behind their global counterparts in achieving the Sustainable Development Goals. However, there are exceptions.

The greatest contribution to the formation of ESG principles is made by exporters of raw materials. The environmental friendliness of the production cycle increases profitability: consumers pay an additional premium for low-carbon raw materials. In particular, the premium for "green" aluminum today reaches 50 US dollars per ton.[47] According to the most authoritative

ESG rating of ESG Morgan Stanley Capital International, only a few companies are leaders in implementing ESG practices in Russia: "Polymetal", "Polyus" and "Novatek" and others.[48]

South Korea is one of the world leaders in building a green economy and in everything related to it. It is obvious that Russia lags far behind South Korea, both in the field of green development methodology and in the field of green technologies. And here there are broad potential prospects for cooperation between our countries. For example, these prospects can be realized within the framework of South Korean North Policy. Russia is also extremely interested in this in order to balance the growing economic and technological influence of China and avoid over-dependence on it.

# From Green Growth to Green Diplomacy:

## Japanese Domestic and International Initiatives Towards a Carbon Neutral Society

## I. Introduction

Speaking at the annual 2021 U.N. Climate Change Conference in Glasgow (COP26) have renewed their commitment to mitigating the global climate crisis, Japanese Prime Minister Kishida Fumio has promised to reduce his country's greenhouse gas (GHG) emissions by 46 percent by 2030 and to net-zero by 2050, while pledging "Japan's strong resolve to exercise leadership toward zero emissions in Asia."[1] To improve its image as a laggard in the fight against climate change,[2] the government has revised Japan's initial goal to meet the 2015 Paris Agreement of the United Nations Framework Convention on Climate Change (UNFCCC) set to cut GHG emissions by 26-28 percent relative to 2013 levels. Kishida's attempt to reclaim Japan's leadership in global climate politics, however, was offset by a "leap backwards" as Tokyo refrained from signing the "Global Coal to Clean Power Transition Statement" which has called on advanced economies to end coal-fired power plants by 2030.[3] In Japan's new basic energy plan approved in October 2021, Kishida has renewed Japan's commitment to coal-fired power plants, which will account for 19 percent of the country's energy mix, while pledging to double the share of renewable energy up to 38 percent. In addition, the new plan has also renewed Japan's commitment to nuclear power, considered "indispensable" achieving the country's decarbonization goals set to meet its commitments made under the Paris Agreement.[4]

Japan ranks fifth in global GHG emissions accounting for a share of 3.2 percent behind top emitters China, the United States, India, and Russia. With 92 percent carbon dioxide accounts for the largest share of Japan's GHG emissions. A large portion of Japan's $CO_2$ emissions are generated in the energy sector, which is dominated by coal, oil and natural gas. Japan's reliance on fossil fuel in energy production is the result of its continued struggle to mitigate the impact of the March 11, 2011 disaster of earthquake and tsunami which caused meltdowns at the Fukushima Daiichi nuclear power plant. With temporary shutdowns of the country's nuclear reactors, economic growth and energy security were maintained through fossil fuels thus resulting in a revival of thermal coal plants. This illustrates how climate and energy policies are entwined. Post-3.11 Japan saw significant changes, including electricity market reforms in form of a feed-in tariff system to promote renewable energies, new grid infrastructure, and a push towards investment in new environmental technology such as hydrogen, and carbon capture and storage. These changes were also driven by an increased influence of non-state actors in climate and energy policymaking, as well as increased international competition over setting new standards to secure national interests in global climate politics and leadership contestation in the Indo-Pacific.

In this chapter, I will review these changes across the domestic and international divide.[5] Domestically, Japan's energy and climate policies are considered the product of an iron-triangle linking corporate interests, a dominant Liberal Democratic Party, and a powerful bureaucracy. The energy market was regulated through close ties between the state and electricity power companies.[6] However, this arrangement came under pressure in the wake of the Fukushima Daiichi nuclear power meltdown. In the following section I will outline path-dependencies and critical junctures that have determined the shifts in Japan's energy and climate policies.


## II. Restoring the status quo

Japan places energy security at the center of its energy policymaking and its response to global climate change politics.[7] In 2003, Japan passed its first Basic Energy Plan (BEP), which sought to further promote nuclear energy, access to stable oil supplies, and energy conservation in line with international climate politics. Later revisions of the BEP adhered to these broad policy goals. In 2007, Japan then introduced a New National Energy

Strategy (NNES), which put a stronger focus on energy security. During his first stint as prime minister, Abe Shinzo in 2007 also introduced a "Cool Earth 50"[8] initiative aiming at reducing Japan's GHG emissions. Following Abe as prime minister, Fukuda Yasuo in 2008 introduced an "Action Plan for Achieving a Low-carbon Society" pledging to cut emissions by 60 to 80 percent by 2050. The plan detailed measures to promote energy efficient housing in line with the new Energy-saving law (2008), a "greener" tax system, promotion of a global environmental tax, investments into environmental business, new rules to reduce carbon footprints, and new environmental technologies such as next-generation vehicles. Yet, this initiative did also call for the "upgrading of coal" and the "promotion of nuclear power" in line with earlier energy planning.[9] In 2010, Japan's government now led by the Democratic Party of Japan (DPJ) revised the country's energy plan. The BEP confirmed Japan's commitment to enhancing energy security, economic efficiency, and environmental sustainability and to boost Japan's "energy independence ratio" to about 70 percent (from 38 percent in 2010). The new plan aimed at a 30 percent reduction of fossil fuel-related $CO_2$ emissions, while doubling the share of renewable energy. To achieve this, the plan proposed an increase of nuclear power to 53 percent by 2030. This target included the construction of 14 new plants in addition to the 54 which were in operation at the time.[10]

Prior to the Fukushima Daiichi meltdown, 26 percent of Japan's energy was generated from nuclear power, 28 percent from liquefied natural gas (LNG), 25 percent from coal, and 13 percent from petroleum, while only

9 percent (including 8 percent hydroelectric power) was generated from renewable energies in 2011.[11] Following Fukushima, Japan was forced to halt all operations at its nuclear power plants. This resulted in an increase of the use of fossil fuels from 65 percent in 2010 to 84 percent in 2016, while GHG emissions increased by 7 percent during the period of 2010 and 2012.[12] In fact, the nuclear meltdown at the Fukushima complex has triggered hopes of a fundamental shift in Japan's energy production to end its dependency on fossil fuel and nuclear energy in favor of promoting renewable energy generation.[13] In 2012, the ruling DPJ did propose the reduction of nuclear power to zero by the 2030s. Prime Minister Kan Naoto also introduced a feed-in tariff (FIT) system to push the country's major electric power companies to expand the market for renewable energy. These measures resulted in an increase in renewable energy production from its previous share of 9 percent to 15 percent in 2016, driven in large part by promotion of new photovoltaic systems.[14]

In addition to the increase in renewable energy, the Fukushima disaster has resulted in new safety regulations for Japan's nuclear industry now overseen by the newly established Nuclear Regulation Authority,[15] and anti-nuclear protest, which made a swift restart of Japan's nuclear power plants difficult. Nevertheless, following his return as prime minister in late 2012, Abe Shinzo and his LDP have pushed for a return to nuclear power. This was in part possible, because the LDP has successfully redirected the debate away from on a focus on the malfunction of the postwar Japanese state's "nuclear village" considered responsible for the lack of safety measures that has resulted in the Fukushima disaster, towards a debate on the crisis of crisis management caused by weak DPJ leadership.[16]

Back in office, Abe in June 2013 adopted the "Japan Revitalization Strategy — Japan is Back,"[17] which has aimed at an average 2 percent real GDP growth during the next decade. The strategy which became known as "Abenomics" called for a restart of nuclear power plants, and low cost and efficient thermal power in form of coal and LNG. This policy was welcomed by Japan's business federation Keidanren which in October 2013 called for the use of fossil fuels, and swift return to nuclear power, as well as abolishment of a tax against global warming. At the same time, renewable energy was considered inadequate to ensure Japan's energy security and economic growth, as non-fossil fuel resources were deemed inefficient, instable, and expensive.[18] In the 2014 BEP, nuclear power was considered crucial for Japan's energy production set to account for 20-22 percent of the energy mix, while planning for renewable energy aimed at a target value of 22-24 percent.[19] In the meantime, Abe in 2016 dramatically revised the FIT-scheme introduced by the DPJ in 2012, thus limiting its impact in promoting renewable energies. In 2016, Japan also decided to decommission the Monju fast-breeder nuclear reactor. Monju was central for Japan's nuclear fuel-cycle, and thus the country's nuclear industry, but despite the investment of over 1 trillion yen since its planning started in 1968, the reactor has not been in operation since 1995 due to technical trouble.[20] Yet, the importance of nuclear energy remained unchanged in the fifth BEP issued in 2018.[21] The target for non-fossil energies including nuclear power was set to 44 percent by 2030. A key initiative under Abe was METI's "Basic Hydrogen Strategy" aiming to promote at least 40000 hydrogen fuel cell vehicles and hydrogen stations by 2020 and in what he termed a "hydrogen society" announced in December 2017.[22]

Yet, despite Abe's rhetoric relating to addressing the climate crisis during Japan's hosting of the G20 summit in 2019, Japan failed to step up in promoting more ambitious targets.[23] A key factor behind this policy shift since 2012 is the central role played by the Ministry of Economy, Trade and Industry (METI) within the policymaking during the Abe era.[24] In what some have called a "METI cabinet," former METI top officials such as Imai Takaya have served as key advisers in Abe's Kantei.[25]

Since the Fukushima disaster, however, energy policymaking has also become more democratized, as subnational actors, courts, and civil society groups have increased their roles vis-à-vis the national government and utilities, which has made it more difficult to implement some of the proposed energy plans such as restarting nuclear power plants or the construction of new coal-fired power plants while urging the government to be more responsive to the agreements reaching in global climate talks, especially after the 2015 Paris Agreement.[26] At the same time, communities have initiated local renewable energy planning and development, with a total of 200 community power enterprises established between 2011 and 2016 alone.[27] This indicates a shift towards a development towards a more decentralized energy sector. At the same time, the private sector has stepped up with its own initiatives. For example, the 2015 established Japan Climate

<Figure 1> Change in Japan's Greenhouse Gas Emissions, 1990-2019

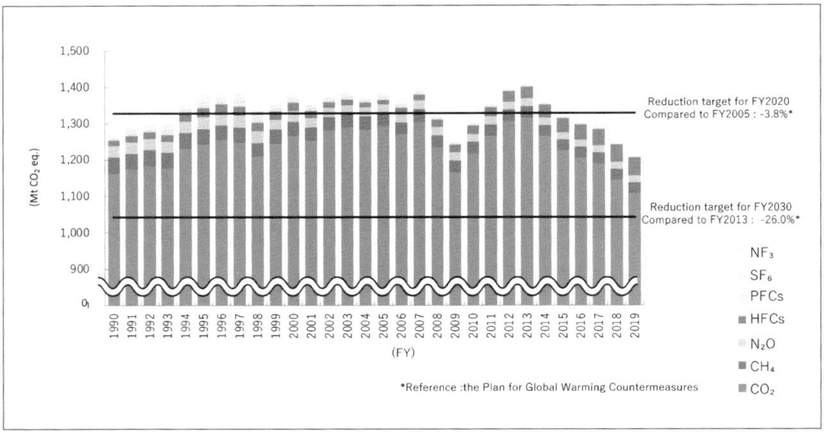

Source: National Institute for Environmental Studies (2021), available at https://www.nies.go.jp/whatsnew/jqjm100000
140x1k-att/jqjm100000140xki.pdf (last accessed February 17, 2022).

Initiative today counts 500 companies (as of February 2022) participating in this scheme which is committed to achieving a carbon-neutral society by 2050 and the goals of the Paris Climate Agreement.[28] Sustainable investment assets quadrupled from 3 percent in 2016 to 18 percent of all professionally managed assets in 2018. As such, Japan has become the third largest market for sustainable investments after Europe and the United States.[29]

In sum, while Japan has succeeded in reducing its GHG emissions from a peak in 2013 (see <Figure 1>), under Abe since 2012 Japan has "backslided" to a current status quo with fossil fuel and nuclear energy at the core of energy production (see <Figure 2>), despite his rhetoric of Japanese leadership in the fight against climate change. Climate and energy policies were placed within the framework of Abenomics. Here, the primary focus was to kick-

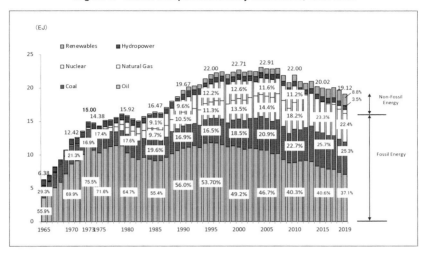

Source: Agency for Natural Resources and Energy, *Energy Whitebook* (2021), available at https://www.enecho.meti.go.jp/about/whitepaper/2020pdf/ (accessed February 17, 2022).

start the Japanese economy through avoiding additional costs on companies and consumers potentially caused by a transition in the energy sector.[30] The primary focus has remained on maximizing energy security and reliable energy supply as the country remains dependent on energy imports. In 2017, Japan's energy self-sufficiency rate was reported at around 9.7 percent and thus down from 20.3 percent in 2010.[31] In July 2020, the Abe government announced shutting down or suspending operation of about 100 low-efficiency coal-fired power plants by 2030. Currently, Japan operates about 140 plants of which 110 are deemed inefficient. At the same time, however, METI announced plans to build 22 new power plants, the nature of which suggesting that Japan's remain committed to fossil-fuel energy.[32] Coal-fired power accounted for 32 percent of the country's total power generation as of 2018, followed by gas-fired generation at 38 percent (<Figure 2>). Yet, during his eight years in office, Abe was able to boost the use of renewable energy to a total of 23.1 percent of the country's energy generation mix and was thus ahead of its target of 22-24 percent by 2030.[33]

## III. From green growth to green diplomacy

In August 2020, Abe suddenly resigned as prime minister and replaced by his long-time Chief Cabinet Secretary Suga Yoshihide. While the period since 2020 has been dominated by the global struggle against the Covid-19 pandemic, some observers predicted a "fundamental shift in approach" to energy policy.[34] During his first address to the Diet, Suga has pledged to reduce GHG emissions to net zero by 2050, and thus revised the previous goal of 80 percent set by the Abe government. As such, Suga made it clear that energy and climate policy will at the center of his administration's agenda.[35] This is the result of Suga's sidelining of METI bureaucrats in his administration as key advisers.[36] At the same time Suga responded to international developments. The European Union in 2019 declared its Green Deal setting the goal to go carbon-free by 2050. Contrary to Japan's course, the UK, France and Germany decided to abolish coal-fired power plants. EU "border tariff adjustments" against countries that do not match EU environmental standards also meant that Japan had to adjust its energy policies if it wanted to avoid putting its businesses at a disadvantage on the European market. Addressing the U.N. General Assembly in September 2020, Chinese leader Xi Jinping proclaimed a "green revolution" for his country setting the goal for "virtually zero emissions" by 2060.[37]

Suga's approach to economic reform ("Suganomics") aimed to creating a virtuous cycle between the economy and the environment to create a "green society" and Japan to "aim to be a carbon-neutral, decarbonized society" by 2050.[38] Suga declared that measures to combat global warming "are not a constraint on economic growth," and that "[w] e need to change our thinking and realize that structural changes in industry and society will lead to significant growth." He also said that Japan will "fundamentally change its policy on coal-fired power generation."[39] To achieve this goal, in December 2020, Suga announced 2 trillion yen to promote research into decarbonization technology over the next decade. His energy agenda was also framed as key for promoting economic growth in the post-coronavirus era. In line with Abe, Suga also promoted hydrogen as a new power source as he pledged to support development of low-cost storage batteries which are key to electric cars, renewable energy, and carbon-recycling technology. In addition, he also pledged zero $CO_2$ emissions from automobiles, through promoting new systems and regulations to promote electric vehicles in Japan.[40]

Marking the beginning of his "green diplomacy," in December 2020 Suga then announced that he will consider attending a global climate summit proposed by Biden. This would be the first bilateral environmental talks since a similar meeting was hosted under the Obama administer in 2015. Following his election in 2020 Biden revised the US's course by rejoining the Paris Agreement, while initiating coordination of national policies to achieve carbon-neutrality by 2050. Suga declared that carbon neutrality "is absolutely necessary for Japan to catch up to global trends and to get one step ahead." Even prior to the US-Japan initiative, in November 2020 Japanese Foreign Minister Motegi Toshimitsu and his Chinese counterpart Wang Yi agreed to launch consultation framework on climate change.[41]

Furthermore, Japan has joined Australia and ASEAN nations to reduce the environmental impact caused by liquefied natural gas supply. Japan is the largest consumer of LNG accounting for 20 percent of the global consumption. Japan has announced that it will promote capture and storage technology to reduce $CO_2$ emissions in the process of LNG production as well as commercializing zero-emission ships for the transport of LNG.[42] On April 22-23, Suga joined Biden's Leaders Summit on Climate initiating the US-Japan Climate Partnership to accelerate transition towards a decarbonized society.[43] Even prior to Biden's election, in July 2020 Japan committed itself to phasing-out 100 old coal-fired power plants by 2030.[44] Following Biden's election in November 2020 Toshiba announced its decision to stop taking orders for building new coal-fired power plants.[45]

The Suga administration has indicated a "return to pragmatism" in Japan's energy policy, which linked green growth and green diplomacy initiatives.[46] In preparation of revising the Basic Energy Plan, in July 2021, METI announced its new plan to increase renewable energy to 36-38 percent by

2030.[47] The previous target that was set in 2018 accounted for share of renewable energy of 22-24 percent by 2030. At the same time, nuclear power was kept at 20 and 22 percent of Japan's overall energy production. The plan was scheduled for approval in October 2021.

After Suga has suddenly resigned in September, energy became a key item in the race for his replacement and the general elections later in 2021.[48] Kishida Fumio's election as LDP chief signaled a return to the politics of Abe and his emphasis on nuclear energy. This shift is marked by officials with ties to the pro-nuclear METI retaking top posts within the party and the government.[49] Hagiuda Koichi who became Japan's minister for Minister of Economy, Trade and Industry (METI) in 2021 explained that nuclear power is "indispensable" to decarbonizing Japan, pledging that "[w]e will work to restart Japan's nuclear reactors."[50] Kishida announced a significant increase in investment, with METI promoting research on next generation nuclear technology including small modular reactors.[51]

In January 2022, Kishida instructed his cabinet to draw up a new clean energy strategy to achieve a carbon neutral society. Here, Kishida promotes nuclear energy and renewable energies as key elements of his "new capitalism" platform.[52] Yet, Kishida's policy of returning to nuclear power so far has made no mention of building new nuclear plants. Japan's existing reactors are all set to reach the end of their 60-year life span by 2060.[53] In addition, Japan Atomic Energy Agency and Mitsubishi Heavy Industries have announced their intention to participate in the U.S.-led development of fast reactors, with potential synergy effects for Japan's domestic nuclear power industry.[54]

At the COP26 summit, Kishida refrained from signing the statement to end coal-fired plants, drawing international criticism. Instead, Japan aims at using low-carbon ammonia to drop $CO_2$ emissions through its "clean coal" approach.[55] The Kishida administration has promised that Japan will fund $100 million worth of projects through the Asia Energy Transition Initiative. During his tour through Southeast Asia in January 2022, METI minister Hagiuda initiated new cooperation with Singapore, Thailand, and Indonesia to further promote the use of ammonia and hydrogen fuel.[56] Doubts nonetheless remain over Kishida's approach focusing on "advanced clean coal technology" as critics point to high costs and low sustainability. To meet Japan's 2050 target of zero-emissions, Japan should instead invest in clean renewable energy.[57]

## IV. Conclusion

In this chapter, I have reviewed recent changes in Japan's energy and climate policies. The period after the Fukushima meltdown was marked by a political push for a return to nuclear energy as a source in Japan's energy mix despite public opposition. At the same time, Japan has made advances in increasing renewable energies. Under Abe, energy and climate policies were approached within the framework of Abenomics, thus avoiding heavy burdens on businesses and consumers caused by drastic shifts in energy production. In this regard, the Suga administration must be considered a critical juncture with its goal of a net-zero emission society and push for more renewable energy, now stressing the positive effects of green growth for Japan's economic development. At the same time, Japan has engaged in active green diplomacy. This change is the result of two major developments: first, Suga's sidelining of pro-nuclear METI officials in his cabinet; and second, the attempt to secure Japan's role in international climate politics and rule setting in the face of new climate initiatives from the EU, China and the U.S.. Under Kishida, Japan's overall energy and climate policy goals remain largely unchanged, with carbon-neutrality now at the core of Kishida's "new capitalism" agenda. Yet, in addition to its push for hydrogen technology, Japan remains committed to coal and nuclear energy in its long-term strategy to cutting emissions, betting on new clean coal and reactor technology. As Japan's industry has already shifted towards more sustainable production, the pressure on Kishida to accelerate his country's energy shift will increase.[58]

During the decade since 3.11 energy and climate policies have become entrenched in Japanese politics. This is in large part the result of enhanced civil society activities, mainly in form of anti-nuclear protests.[59] According to recent Japanese government surveys, more than 88 percent of the public are interested in global climate issues, while 84 percent claim to have knowledge of the Paris Agreement. More than 68 percent have stated they know about the concept of a "carbon-neutral society."[60] This clearly illustrates that recent debates about energy and climate policies have generated large public interest and thus that recent policy discourses have succeeded in entrenching this issue in the political discourse. In fact, as new scholarship has pointed out, it was only in 2020 that Japan's environmental ministry introduced the term "climate crisis" in Japan's energy and climate policy discourse and that Japan's Diet has issued a "climate emergency declaration," illustrating a shift towards the "securitization" of the climate discourse in Japan.[61] This process will likely continue as energy and climate politics are now part of Japan's regional security strategy in its bid for leadership in the Indo-Pacific in the form of its "Free and Open Indo Pacific" (FOIP) vision. As such, the September 2021 Quadrilateral Security Dialogue (QUAD) has actively addressed the issue of climate change.[62] This emphasis was reiterated at the QUAD foreign ministers' meeting in February 2022.[63] In fact, Japan's emphasis on energy and climate cooperation in Asia stated at the COP26 summit further illustrates the increased role that this issue has come to play in the Kishida administration's regional security strategy.

# Estimation of Sewerage Level of Service by Disposal Paths of Excreta in North Korea

## I. Introduction

The sewerage, or the sewage system, is crucial not only for maintaining water quality and hygiene but also for preventing flood or other related natural disasters in receiving water bodies. The management of sewerage service of a certain country is affected by the overall level of infrastructure of that country.

The DPRK seems to have maintained the sewerage since its construction. However, due to the economic difficulties, the level of sewerage in North Korea has fluctuated, which makes it difficult for South Korean and foreign scholars to estimate. This paper is an attempt to present a possibly reasonable estimation of North Korea's sewerage service level based on the released data on the disposal paths of excreta.

The North Korean water and sewage systems are known to have been built and installed during the 1960s and 1970s with the support of the Soviet Union. However, with little data on the recent situation on the ground, our knowledge of the sewage system in North Korea is far from sufficient. Even the materials available do not seem to be trustworthy with conflicting data depending on sources, which makes their credibility questionable at best.

Nevertheless, there exist some materials that seem to have relatively high reliability. Some of the DPRK's legislations show North Korea's policies and administration of its sewerage. In 2018, North Korea and UNICEF conducted a survey to find out the recent conditions of the sanitation and the disposal pathways of excrement in North Korea. The result of that particular survey helps us figure out the recent situation in North Korea and estimate their sewage system service level. Another important source for estimating the service level of the sewage system of North Korea is the college textbook titled *the Sewerage Engineering*. Published in 2015, this book, which foreign scholars could obtain with relative ease, reveals what kind of education is being offered in North Korea as well as the goals of that education pursued by the DPRK. The book also contains the references and bibliography of the materials used by the authors. Hence, based on these materials and literature, one may glimpse at the situations of the current sewage system in North Korea.

## II. Laws and Regulations regarding the Sewerage in North Korea

There are several laws and regulations governing the sewage systems in North Korea, showing the basic concept of the sewerage as well as details about how to manage wastewater and what measures are taken to control the sewer system and services. For examples, DPRK's Environmental Protection Act (2014), which covers not only treatment of wastewater but also the construction of waste treatment plants. A law titled The Sewerage Act (2009), which was enacted much earlier, includes some provisions and regulations that mandate purification and treatment of wastewater (<Table 1>). Another

<Table 1> The Schema of the DPRK's Sewerage Act (2009)

| Chapter and Article | Contents |
| --- | --- |
| Chapter 1. The Basic Concepts of the Sewerage Law (Article 1-8) | The Purpose and Definition of the Law; the principles of construction and modernization of the sewerage; the principles of disposal of excreta; the principles of preservation of the sewerage; scientific research; the education of experts and engineers |
| Chapter 2. The Construction of the Sewerage (Article 9-15) | The planning and designing of the sewerage construction; the requirements of construction; the connection of pipes; the complete inspection of construction |
| Chapter 3. The Management of the Sewerage (Article 16-29) | The registration and control of the sewerage facilities; the administration's responsibilities; the maintenance and inspection; the disposal of expired facilities |
| Chapter 4. The Treatment of the Wastewater (Article 30-37) | The purification and sanitation of wastewater; the inspection of water quality; the treatment of domestic and industrial wastewater; the treatment of rainwater |
| Chapter 5. The Instruction and Control of the Sewerage (Article 38-43) | The administrative guidance and direction; The reparation and compensation; The legal and administrative responsibilities |

important set of legislations are The Urban Management Act (2015), which governs sewage systems of North Korea's urban areas, and the Pyongyang City Management Act (1998), which regulates the management of the capital city, Pyongyang. The Infectious Disease Prevention Law (2005) also touches upon the wastewater treatment and its processing, which are important in preventing infectious diseases. Provisions that regulate sanitization or sterilization of pits and waste treatment facilities are included in that law.

In terms of rights and responsibilities of local governments, the central government is the one that constructs sewerage, while local governments are actually in charge of managing or operating sewage systems. According to The Pyongyang City Management Act, it is evident that DPRK pays particular attention on the sewerage of Pyongyang City. The law includes provisions that address both water supply and sewage systems. Since Taedong river, beside which the North Korean capital city is located, is considered one of the most important rivers in North Korea, the DPRK also maintains a regulation called The Taedong River Pollution Prevention Act (2005). This act contains some provisions about how to process and treat wastewater, how to prevent oil spills, and how to dispose medical or chemical substances.

When it comes to the administrative bodies that govern the management of the environment as well as the sewage systems of DPRK, no information has been revealed yet regarding the distribution of responsibilities. However, following the national territory planning for each province and sub-planning for each city and small county, these administrative bodies in the plan are believed to be responsible for managing and running sewage systems in the regions under their jurisdiction. Accordingly, the city governments would report to the provincial level governments about their operating and managing the sewage system. Then, provinces would in turn report to the central government.

The service level of the sewage system in DPRK may be estimated through the analysis of the published materials. In particular, the book titled *The Sewerage Engineering*, which was written for college education, includes some chapters that discuss the sewerage operation and management as well as constructing and designing storm or sanitary sewer pipes. The contents show that North Koreans consider hydrologic factors of rainfall intensity, duration, and frequency. In addition, the book gives us some insight on North Korea's notion of employing various types of methods for the treatment of wastewater. There are some highly sophisticated purification methods explained in that book, which are those quite commonly used in South Korea and other developed countries as well.

Among the advanced professional methods introduced in the textbook, the chapter ten deserves our attention because it addresses small-scale Decentralized Wastewater Treatment Systems. This particular technology is not necessarily used in cities. The concept of small scale decentralized wastewater treatment is more common in rural areas where a population is relatively small. The DPRK seems to take it seriously and attempt to apply the technology as demonstrated in the textbook.

Another part that attracts our attention is the list of references that were used to publish the college textbook. About 10 books or literature were referenced, and most of them were from Chinese and Russian literature. An English titled book was published in Germany. Therefore, one can conclude that most of the references of the Sewerage Engineering were based upon the scientific accomplishment made in socialist countries or in Germany.

When it comes to urban planning and the designing of sewage system in North Korea, we need to consider demographic composition or demographic changes. North Korea currently has over twenty million population with two million population residing in Pyongyang. Hamhung, Nampo and Sunchon have populations around 400,000 to 500,000. Only a few cities have the population over 300,000. Based on the relatively low level of urbanization, the population seems quite dispersed across the country in North Korea.

According to the existing literature regarding North Korea's sewage system, many experts have already pointed out that Pyongyang city particularly has its own sewage treatment plants though no literature has commented exactly how many sewage treatment plants are located in Pyongyang. Depending on studies, the number of treatment plants in Pyongyang is counted differently. A study argues that there are three sewage treatment plants in Pyongyang city. Nevertheless, due to economic difficulties and shortage of electricity in North Korea, it is uncertain that all those plants are in operation. Consequently, the wastewater may not be sufficiently or properly treated, which could lead to the pollution of the Taedong river.

With regard to the rate of population connected to sewage treatment facility, it is usually calculated based on the number of people living in a specified region and how many people actually have access to sewer pipes and then sewage treatment facility. Although it is very difficult to make an estimation about the exact rate of population connected to sewage treatment facility, it has thus far been suggested that about 93 percent of the population in South Korea has had access to sewer pipes and sewage treatment facility. However, in rural areas, fewer people have direct access to sophisticated sewer pipes, which in effect compound the problem.

In 2008, based on the data released by international organization, Zuhwan Yun published a study on the rate of population connected to sewage treatment facility in North Korea. Yun argues that when looking at the disposal paths of excreta, one may find about 80 percent of the North Korean population actually use the method of open defecation. In effect, there remain some places where neither toilet nor latrine was built, which reminds us of the situation in Seoul in the 1950s before the sewage system was built. Given those conditions, the wastewater treatment rate is clearly different from the common definition of the percentage of population connected to sewage treatment facility.

Regarding the wastewater treatment rate in North Korea, the figure of about 19.5% was presented in 2008. However, this estimation lacks evidence. On the other hand, according to the data gathered and released by UNICEF in 2018, the situation seems quite different from what experts thought ten years ago. As UNICEF actually conducted the survey on the topic with the support of the North Korean government in 2017, the results appear more reliable with the 8,500 households surveyed. As can be seen from <Table 2>, the treatment rate was estimated to be 56.9%, which shows impressive improvement if we accept Zuhwan Yun's estimation of 17.5% as true. Although the estimation of 2017 is considered more credible than that of 2008, it is still too hasty to judge the 2017 survey shows the exact reality of the sewerage in North Korea because of the limited number of samples.

<Table 2> Excrement Treatment by Urban and Rural Areas

| Year | | 2008[*] | 2017[**] |
|------|------|------|------|
| Flush/Pour flush | Piped sewer system | 13.6% | 44.6% |
| | Septic tank | 2.6% | 9.6% |
| | Pit latrine | 3.3% | 2.7% |
| | **Treatment Rate** | **19.5%** | **56.9%** |
| No flush | Pit latrine improved with ventilation or slab | 79.7% | 27.2% |
| | Open pit or drain | 0.8% | 15.9% |
| | **No Treatment** | **80.5%** | **43.1%** |

Source: [*]Yun(2008): [**]DPRK and UNICEF (2018)

To classify into urban areas and rural areas, as one can see from <Table 3>, the wastewater treatment rate for urban areas is found to reach 75.5%, while the rural areas show only the wastewater treatment rate of 27.9 percent. This difference is created from the fact that people in rural areas still have the custom of disposing of excreta without treatment.

<Table 3> Excrement Treatment by Urban and Rural Areas

| Urban and Rural | | Total | Urban | Rural |
|---|---|---|---|---|
| Flush/Pour flush | Piped sewer system | 44.6% | 67.2% | 9.5% |
| | Septic tank | 9.6% | 6.4% | 14.5% |
| | Pit latrine | 2.7% | 1.9% | 3.9% |
| | **Treatment Rate** | **56.9%** | **75.5%** | **27.9%** |
| No flush | Pit latrine improved with ventilation or slab | 27.2% | 16.2% | 44.5% |
| | Open pit or drain | 15.9% | 8.4% | 27.7% |
| | **No Treatment** | **43.1%** | **24.6%** | **72.2%** |

Source: DPRK and UNICEF (2018)

An analysis of excrement treatment by region (<Table 4>) presents another stark contrast between the capital city Pyongyang and other regions. In Pyongyang, the wastewater treatment rate rises over 90%. By contrast, average rate of treatment in other regions remain below the national average of 56.9%. When looking at the numbers by province, Northern Hamgyong and Jagang mark the relatively high wastewater treatment rates of more than 50 percent, while Southern Hwanghae province shows the lowest treatment rate.

<Table 4> Excrement Treatment by Region

| | Provinces and Capital | Ryanggang | North Hamgyong | South Hamgyong | Kangwon | Jagang | North Pyongan | South Pyongan | North Hwanghae | South Hwanghae | Pyongyang |
|---|---|---|---|---|---|---|---|---|---|---|---|
| Flush/ Pour Flush | Piped Sewer system | 23.9 | 45.1 | 35.9 | 33.9 | 57.4 | 45.9 | 43.4 | 29.9 | 28.2 | 83.2 |
| | Septic tank | 25.7 | 18.2 | 18.0 | 10.9 | 5.2 | 5.0 | 2.9 | 10.8 | 5.5 | 6.7 |
| | Pit latrine | 0.0 | 0.4 | 1.0 | 3.7 | 0.1 | 0.0 | 4.3 | 13.0 | 1.4 | 0.4 |
| | Treatment Rate | **49.6** | **63.7** | **54.9** | **48.5** | **62.7** | **50.9** | **50.6** | **53.7** | **35.1** | **90.3** |
| No Flush | Pit latrine improved with ventilation or slab | 35.1 | 24.4 | 29.8 | 33.8 | 17.0 | 28.8 | 30.3 | 31.2 | 38.2 | 8.5 |
| | Open pit | 15.3 | 11.8 | 15.2 | 17.6 | 20.3 | 20.3 | 19.0 | 15.0 | 26.7 | 1.3 |
| | No Treatment | **50.4** | **36.2** | **45.0** | **51.4** | **37.3** | **49.1** | **49.3** | **46.2** | **64.9** | **9.8** |

Source: DPRK and UNICEF (2018)

UNICEF research includes a study that shows whether the excreta are being safely disposed or unsafely disposed. There are cases that disposal of excreta is made from on-site sanitation. However, in most cases, excreta are being disposed of unsafely, ending up being used as compost fertilizers in farm lands. Of course, they might include some nutrients that could be good for the soil, but there can be also pollutants that would flow into water sources, which could actually lead to a rise or outbreak of infectious diseases as well as the contamination of drinking water. Therefore, from the perspectives of environmental preservation and hygiene, it is crucial to keep an eye on whether and how the treatment of excreta will be developed and improved in North Korea.

In general, the North Korean sewerage remains less sophisticated than those of other countries. However, as a new water management paradigm arises, it seems that North Koreans take it seriously and begin to emphasize it. To explain the new paradigm, it is necessary to compare it with the existing water management paradigms. In the past, the focus was placed on the construction of wastewater treatment and sewer pipes used to collect sewage, which has been widely used in establishing cities by human beings for a long time. This paradigm has been considered as basic infrastructure for large cities.

Recently, the new concept of small-scale decentralized wastewater treatment system is gaining foothold, and more and more people are arguing for and advocating for the decentralized water management. The advantage that the small-scale decentralized wastewater treatment system draws much attention is that it can be run with less cost and energy while other environment friendly technologies can be applied to it.

Interestingly enough, the paradigm shift has been adopted by North Koreans, who have already started to discuss this topic when managing their sewer systems. North Korea has been emphasizing maintenance and operation technologies that include automation technologies to operate the wastewater treatment plants and roll out the decentralized small scale purification structures. Despite lingering economic difficulties, North Korea seems to be eager to adopt the newly rising trend in the sewerage system, which is drawing attention of the international discussion.

Nevertheless, the small-scale decentralized wastewater treatment system could cause problems threatening public health without proper care made for its management. If the sewer system based on the concept of small-scale decentralized wastewater treatment system failed, it could lead to a rise or outbreak of infectious diseases. North Korea may want to move toward the new paradigm because its suggestion for the new idea could arouse interest and possibly receive support from the international community. If North Korea successfully built its new water management system by adopting the small-scale decentralized wastewater treatment sewage system paradigm, it would be a good example that proves the effectiveness of the small-scale decentralized wastewater treatment system.

# III. Conclusion

This paper presents the most reasonable estimation on the rate of sewage treatment and the effectiveness of the sewerage of North Korea based on the published and released data.

As analyzed above, the total rate of sewage treatment of North Korea in 2017 was estimated to be 56.9%. The rate in urban areas was 75.5%, whereas the rate in the countryside 27.9%, which indicates the considerable gap in sewage level of service between cities and other areas. As for the regional difference, North Hamgyong Province marked the highest 63.7%, Jagang the second 62.7%, and South Hwanghae Province had the lowest 35.1%. In general, the rate of unsafe sewage treatment was very high because the great amount of excrement amounting to 89~92% was estimated to be used as fertilizer in North Korea. Such a custom could lead to the contamination of drinking water and the outbreak of waterborne infectious diseases. Without resources to modernize their sewerage, North Korea seems to promote the expansion of the small-scale decentralized wastewater treatment system. However, this policy, based on different premises from those of the West, might lead to the disruption of water supply and quicken the deterioration of sanitation level in North Korea.

# An Overview of Natural Disasters in North Korea and Inter-Korean Cooperation Strategies

## I. Introduction

Addressing natural disasters has become a crucial topic because the climate change brings about more powerful natural disasters more often than before. Various global and regional initiatives are taken not just by the governments but also by international organizations. Cooperation among them is necessary to share information, provide mutual aid, and coordinate efforts to prevent natural disasters and to deal with damages caused by those unprecedently strong natural events.

*   This paper was written following the research work "A Study on the Environmental Status in North Korea and the Development of Inter-Korean Environmental Cooperation"(GP2021-13), funded by the Korea Environment Institute (KEI).

Cooperation between North and South Korea to tackle natural disasters is of great importance particularly because both Koreas, located in the Korean Peninsula, often face natural disasters at the same time and share the damage from the same natural disasters. Above all, with the great possibilities that such a cooperation may bring in the process of building peace in the region, the governments of the two Koreas have been interested in materializing cooperation for addressing natural disasters. However, it is also true that inter-Korean cooperation sometimes took form of political competition between the two different political systems, democratic South and communist North. When one fell victim of a natural disaster, the other would use it to demonstrate its superiority by providing generous aid.

Based upon one of the projects being conducted by the Center for Environmental Information of North Korea at Korea Environment Institute, this paper is aimed to examine what kind of natural disasters have recently happened in North Korea, how much they have caused damages, and how South Korea and North Korean would seek cooperation to address natural disasters.

## II. Natural Disasters in North Korea: Recent Trend

Although the DPRK has taken firm control of the media since its establishment, the news about the natural disasters, which are created first and foremost for domestic purpose of informing North Korean people, have been released outside through various means of broadcast either by accident or on purpose. The reason for the DPRK's permission to circulate the news about the occurrence of natural disasters is obvious: they want to let other countries know about the effects of the natural disasters. Consequently, South Koreans can notice when and what kinds of natural disasters happen in North Korea. Recent press reports about natural disasters in North Korea indicate that the DPRK faces serious challenges in responding to the increasingly strong natural disasters.

According to the Global Risk Index 2020, which was published by the Europe Union, North Korea is ranked about 39th place in terms of vulnerability to the risks of natural disasters. However, the situation seems deteriorating. Index for Risk Management 2021 Report ranked North Korea to the 29th place out of 191 countries around the world.

According to other data, including FAO's *Agricultural Production Situation in DPR Korea*: 2020, natural disasters' impact on the crop harvest was enormous. In the provinces of North and South Hwanghae, which are known as the granary in North Korea and make up the high proportion of rice and corn production, the crop yield has dropped by a considerable degree due to the flood damage over 20,000 hectares. The report also offers a future scenario that predicts the further deterioration of food crop. Shortages of food has a negative impact on nutrition of people, especially children, leading to another serious problem lingering across North Korea.

Natural disasters in North Korea have taken heavy tolls on human beings along with damages on property. One of the most serious kinds of natural disaster that North Korea has undergone is flood. In summer and fall, typhoons and heavy rain often result in inundation. Flooding not just affects arable lands in North Korea, which causes shortages of food, but also leads to deforestation and the destruction of infrastructure, such as the water supply and sewage systems. Since North Korea's water system remains poor in quality, a flood in North Korea is likely to lead to the failure of the water supply and the sewerage, which could adversely affect drinking water and wreak havoc to the hygiene and safety of the North Korean people by causing the outbreak of infectious diseases.

The Center for Environmental Information on North Korea at KEI has published a series of reports on Natural disasters in North Korea, including the following table of the occurrence of natural disasters in the past 30 years from 1991 to 2020. (<Table 1>) These data were compiled based on reports that have been reported by North Korea and the international organizations as well as news released both in North Korea and South Korea.

<Table 1> Natural Disasters in North Korea (1991-2020) (Numbers)

| Year | Typhoon | Flood | Heavy Downpour | Strong wind | High Waves | Tsunami | Heavy Snow | Lightning | Drought | Earthquake** | Yellow Dust | Algae Blooming | High Tide | Volcano Activity | Extreme Cold | Extreme Heat | Rock Falls | Total (Simultaneous Occasions)* |
|---|---|---|---|---|---|---|---|---|---|---|---|---|---|---|---|---|---|---|
| '91 | 0 | 0 | 1 | 1 | 0 | 0 | 0 | 0 | 1 | 0 | 0 | 0 | 0 | 0 | 0 | 0 | 0 | 3 |
| '92 | 0 | 0 | 0 | 0 | 0 | 0 | 0 | 0 | 1 | 1 | 0 | 0 | 0 | 0 | 0 | 0 | 0 | 2 |
| '93 | 1 | 0 | 0 | 0 | 0 | 2 | 0 | 0 | 0 | 0 | 0 | 0 | 0 | 0 | 0 | 0 | 0 | 3(1) |
| '94 | 0 | 0 | 0 | 0 | 0 | 0 | 0 | 0 | 1 | 1 | 0 | 0 | 0 | 0 | 0 | 1 | 0 | 3 |
| '95 | 1 | 2 | 3 | 1 | 0 | 0 | 0 | 0 | 0 | 0 | 0 | 0 | 0 | 0 | 0 | 0 | 0 | 7(2) |
| '96 | 0 | 2 | 1 | 0 | 0 | 0 | 0 | 0 | 0 | 0 | 0 | 0 | 0 | 0 | 0 | 0 | 0 | 3(1) |
| '97 | 1 | 2 | 1 | 0 | 0 | 1 | 0 | 0 | 1 | 0 | 0 | 0 | 0 | 0 | 0 | 1 | 0 | 7(1) |
| '98 | 0 | 1 | 6 | 3 | 0 | 1 | 0 | 0 | 1 | 1 | 0 | 0 | 0 | 0 | 0 | 0 | 0 | 13(3) |
| '99 | 2 | 1 | 1 | 0 | 0 | 0 | 0 | 0 | 1 | 1 | 0 | 0 | 0 | 0 | 0 | 0 | 0 | 6(1) |
| '00 | 1 | 0 | 0 | 0 | 0 | 0 | 0 | 0 | 1 | 0 | 0 | 0 | 0 | 0 | 0 | 1 | 0 | 3 |
| '01 | 0 | 1 | 2 | 1 | 0 | 1 | 2 | 0 | 2 | 0 | 1 | 0 | 0 | 0 | 1 | 1 | 2 | 14(5) |
| '02 | 3 | 1 | 3 | 2 | 0 | 1 | 0 | 0 | 0 | 4 | 3 | 0 | 0 | 0 | 0 | 0 | 1 | 18(7) |
| '03 | 0 | 0 | 1 | 0 | 0 | 0 | 0 | 0 | 0 | 0 | 0 | 0 | 0 | 0 | 0 | 0 | 1 | 2(1) |
| '04 | 1 | 2 | 5 | 0 | 0 | 0 | 0 | 0 | 0 | 0 | 8 | 0 | 0 | 0 | 1 | 0 | 1 | 18(4) |
| '05 | 1 | 1 | 4 | 1 | 0 | 2 | 0 | 0 | 0 | 0 | 8 | 0 | 0 | 0 | 0 | 0 | 1 | 18(6) |
| '06 | 0 | 2 | 3 | 1 | 0 | 1 | 0 | 0 | 0 | 0 | 1 | 0 | 0 | 0 | 0 | 0 | 2 | 10(6) |
| '07 | 1 | 1 | 2 | 1 | 0 | 0 | 0 | 0 | 0 | 0 | 4 | 0 | 0 | 0 | 0 | 0 | 0 | 9(3) |
| '08 | 1 | 1 | 1 | 1 | 0 | 0 | 0 | 0 | 0 | 0 | 1 | 0 | 0 | 0 | 1 | 0 | 0 | 5(3) |
| '09 | 0 | 0 | 1 | 0 | 0 | 0 | 0 | 0 | 0 | 0 | 0 | 0 | 0 | 0 | 1 | 0 | 1 | 3(1) |

| Year | Typhoon | Flood | Heavy Downpour | Strong wind | High Waves | Tsunami | Heavy Snow | Lightning | Drought | Earthquake** | Yellow Dust | Algae Blooming | High Tide | Volcano Activity | Extreme Cold | Extreme Heat | Rock Falls | Total (Simultaneous Occasions) * |
|---|---|---|---|---|---|---|---|---|---|---|---|---|---|---|---|---|---|---|
| '10 | 1 | 4 | 4 | 2 | 0 | 0 | 0 | 0 | 0 | 0 | 0 | 0 | 0 | 0 | 2 | 0 | 0 | 13(7) |
| '11 | 2 | 2 | 5 | 2 | 0 | 1 | 2 | 0 | 1 | 0 | 11 | 0 | 0 | 0 | 1 | 0 | 1 | 28(8) |
| '12 | 2 | 5 | 5 | 1 | 0 | 0 | 0 | 0 | 1 | 0 | 0 | 0 | 0 | 0 | 2 | 0 | 2 | 18(10) |
| '13 | 0 | 1 | 1 | 0 | 0 | 0 | 0 | 0 | 0 | 0 | 0 | 0 | 0 | 0 | 1 | 0 | 1 | 4(2) |
| '14 | 0 | 0 | 0 | 0 | 0 | 0 | 0 | 0 | 1 | 0 | 1 | 0 | 0 | 0 | 0 | 0 | 0 | 2(0) |
| '15 | 1 | 2 | 2 | 0 | 0 | 1 | 0 | 0 | 1 | 0 | 0 | 0 | 0 | 0 | 0 | 0 | 0 | 7(4) |
| '16 | 1 | 2 | 4 | 0 | 0 | 0 | 0 | 0 | 0 | 1 | 1 | 0 | 0 | 0 | 0 | 2 | 1 | 12(2) |
| '17 | 0 | 0 | 1 | 0 | 0 | 0 | 0 | 0 | 1 | 0 | 0 | 0 | 0 | 0 | 0 | 0 | 0 | 2 |
| '18 | 1 | 3 | 2 | 1 | 0 | 0 | 0 | 0 | 0 | 0 | 0 | 0 | 0 | 0 | 1 | 1 | 0 | 9(3) |
| '19 | 2 | 3 | 3 | 2 | 0 | 1 | 0 | 0 | 1 | 2 | 0 | 0 | 0 | 0 | 0 | 0 | 0 | 14(3) |
| '20 | 4 | 2 | 4 | 2 | 0 | 1 | 0 | 0 | 2 | 1 | 0 | 0 | 0 | 0 | 0 | 0 | 0 | 16(4) |
| 총계 | 27 | 41 | 66 | 22 | 0 | 13 | 4 | 0 | 17 | 14 | 39 | 0 | 0 | 0 | 10 | 7 | 14 | 272(88) |

* When a natural disaster continued for two months with some aftermaths, only the first occurrence was counted.
** Only earthquakes over 3.5 on Richter Scale were counted. In the event of earthquake happening in the sea, only the one that can be located were counted.

According to the data, the total of 272 occasions of natural disaster have hit North Korea over thirty years. Categorizing them into the decades, 50 happened in the 1990s, whereas 222 occurred in the 2010s, showing an increase in the frequency of natural disaster. Dividing them into several categories, there were 88 events that actually took place at the same time. Some natural disasters are seasonal: the freezing damage and frost often occur between December and February, yellow dust between March and May, drought in Jun, and flooding accompanied by heavy downpour from July to October. The earthquake with the magnitude of 3.5 on the Richter Magnitude Scale or higher, which can be felt by the human beings, took place 14 times in North Korea.

Sorting the occasions of natural disasters in North Korea by region, as can be seen in <Figure 1>, one can find out that most of the natural disasters tend to occur across the border areas with South Korea. By contrast, natural disasters that broke out in Ryanggang or other northern provinces have been less reported by the North Korean media. The reason of this contrast might be derived from the fact that the southern areas of North Korea have more populations, whose damages are more likely to be reported in the media. Another possible theory to explain the tendency is that local governments of the border areas are more eager to collect data in the events, including natural resources. On the other hand, the northern provinces, which usually consist of mountainous regions, are likely to have less population compared to those near the inter-Korean border. Perhaps, natural disasters in the northern areas might have happened at the same frequency with the south.

<Figure 1> Natural Disaster Occurrence by Region

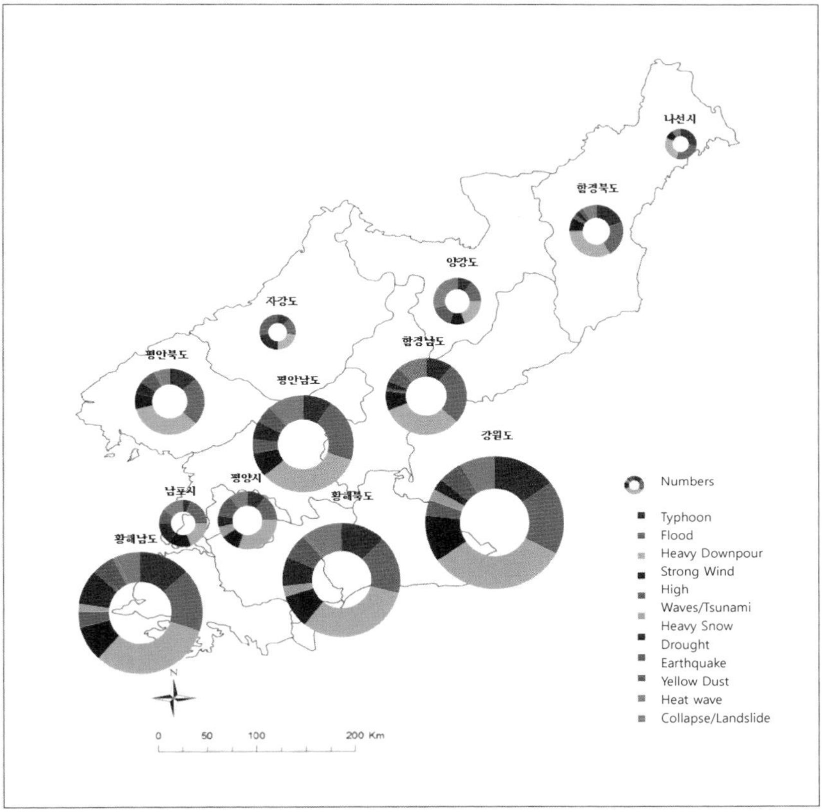

## III. North Korea's Responses to Natural Disasters

Under Kim Jong Un's leadership, it seems that the DPRK has made greater efforts to address natural disasters. North Korean newspaper reports have more frequently released the scenes that show Chairman Kim Jong Un actually coming to the site of the natural disaster, wearing a shirt and giving instructions to the local authorities about how to handle the aftermath of the natural disaster. As those scenes appear in the North Korean media more frequently compared to the previous North Korean leaders, it can be assumed that there seems to be a greater interest in the North Korea leadership in responding to natural disasters. Due to such changing perception, more North Korean radio or tv broadcasting has been released in order to let people know about the natural disasters. Such an attitude change gives more chance for South Korean and international watchers to gain more information through North Korean media coverage on the sites than in the past. For example, the heavy rainfall in August, 2021, was so widely covered in North Korea's media that South Koreans also came to know about it well through their own news media, which cited North Korea's broadcast.

The DPRK also seems to become more interested in building systems to respond to the natural disasters. Although only limited information is available, it is known that under the central cabinet of the DPRK, a new bureau named National Emergency, Natural Prevention and Response Committee has recently been established. This particular committee is referred to by different names depending on the media outlets, but it is considered that there must be a single body to coordinate governmental response to natural disasters. More precise judgement regarding this bureaus' role and responsibilities will be possible only after more integrated information becomes available.

Another crucial evidence for change in North Korea's attitude on dealing with natural disasters is that the DPRK attempts to follow the international community's methods of responding to natural disasters. For example, the DPRK published in 2019 its natural disaster risk reduction strategy. In addition, the North Korean government voluntarily published a national review. All of those efforts show North Korea's commitment to building up their capability for responding to natural disasters while achieving Sustainable Development Goals in alignment with the trend of the international community because the DPRK declared its voluntary will to actually reduce greenhouse gases. In 2018, North Korea established sustainable development national task force, which will cover sustainable development in general.

However, North Korea still has only limited resources and infrastructure for responding to natural resources. It also remains overdependent on external institutions like international organizations. The DPRK's response to natural disasters still remains to be determined by its leader Kim Jong Un's instructions and guidance rather than to be carried out through a system. In fact, the DPRK did legislate a law on disaster prevention and restoration in 2014. In order for a legislation to be effective, enforcement ordinances and specific regulations must follow up, yet there is not enough information revealed on whether such ordinances and regulations were prepared or not. Without supporting ordinances and regulation, there seems to be limitation in the enforcement of such legislations.

## IV. International and Inter-Korean Cooperation for Responding to Natural Disasters

The international community as well as South Korea has been deeply involved in responding to natural disasters in North Korea. A number of international NGOs have conducted their activities to meet the needs posed by increasing damage of natural disasters. Natural disasters tend to cause shortage of food, which international organizations have been working to tackle for years. The activities of international organizations have been based on a strategic framework, focusing on four major fields: food and nutrition, social development services, sustainable development, and data and development management.

However, the sanctions imposed against North Korea have placed rigorous restrictions on material support, making it difficult for international organizations to carry out their projects. Furthermore, with the outbreak of the COVID-19 pandemic, those organizations and personnel from the international organizations had to leave North Korea, while some NGOs, particularly under the UN, decided to remain and continue to cooperate with the DPRK in responding to natural disasters amid the pandemic crisis.

From this perspective, inter-Korean cooperation on the field of preventing and responding to natural disasters is of great significance. In fact, South Korea and North Korea have maintained a history of cooperation on natural disaster response although the level of cooperation still remains quite low. The inter-Korean cooperation in terms of natural disaster response had not drawn attention until 1992. In 2000, the two Korean governments started their talk for cooperation. Most of the inter-Korean cooperation in the 2000s focused on prevention of flood damages. After the accident in Imjin River in 2009, when six South Koreans were drowned due to the unannounced discharge of water from the Huanggang dam by the DPRK, the representative of the two Koreas met three times in 2010~2011 and agreed that North Korea would inform South Korea of the discharge of water from the dam in advance. However, the following strain in the inter-Korean relations impeded further talks.

Although there seem to be many obstacles to huddle to resume inter-Korean cooperation, South Korea cannot wait and see but should take an initiative in play a leading role. Natural disasters in North Korea have impacts on the whole Korean Peninsula. The food shortage and disease outbreaks can affect South Korea. Moreover, the humanitarian crisis caused by natural disasters calls on South Koreans to act to reach out to help North Koreans. The North Korean government also considers these natural disasters as critical threats and welcomes international community, which might make it possible that South Korea and North Korea work together to reduce the impact of natural disasters.

Of course, there exists the issue of the sanctions against North Korea because the international community as well as individual countries have sanctions against the DPRK. Nevertheless, there could niches and approaches that we need to think about to realize the inter-Korean cooperation regarding natural disasters. The following may offer a glimpse at possible starting points. First, North Korea still remains to be committed to working to receive aid from international organizations. South Korea may want to collaborate with those international organization to find ways of supporting North Korea in preventing and managing natural disasters. Second, North Korea did reach a number of agreements with South Korea. For example, both Koreas decided to maintain a subcommittee for responding to natural disasters and exchanging related information. In that context, South Korea needs to expand efforts to make the best use of the inter-Korean subcommittee. Third, because natural disasters require approaches from a comprehensive perspective, the inter-Korean cooperation may start from other areas such as food, health, energy, or others. South Korea should consider a holistic approach toward all of these aspects. Fourth, South Korea can start to resolve contradictions in the legal system or the institutional system between the two Koreas. In the environmental fields, some of the laws and regulations are in conflict with each other. Therefore, to materialize any meaningful inter-Korean cooperation, it is necessary to reassess legal and administrative incompatibilities and discuss how to resolve these contradictions. For example, in terms of Certified Emission Reduction(CER), the two Koreas may work together with emission trading, yet the prerequisite adjustments in the legal system must be made to allow this sort of cooperation.

# North Korea's Climate Change and Implications for Inter-Korean Cooperation

## I. Introduction

Climate change is becoming serious around the world. The Intergovernmental Panel on Climate Change (IPCC) has warned that if the current level of greenhouse gas emission continues, the threshold toward the extreme climate crisis will be crossed much earlier than expected. The change of climate is occurring fast in the Korean Peninsula. The data publicized thus far clearly indicates that the average temperature is rising in both South and North Koreas, but more seriously so in North Korea. Climate change has impacts on the frequency and intensity of natural disasters, which cause negative effects on people's lives. Therefore, readiness to respond to climate change is of urgent necessity. To minimize the negative effects of climate change, it is necessary to strengthen the adaptive capacity to climate change while making efforts to reduce the greenhouse gas emission. This paper discusses the current situation of climate change and its impacts on North Korea and explores the possible cooperation measures between South and North Koreas to enhance the response ability to the climate change.

## II. Climate Change in North Korea

Climate change happens globally, including the Korean Peninsula. The average temperature rise is a phenomenon commonly found in the whole Korean Peninsula. According to a study conducted by the National Institute of Meteorological Sciences (2018) (<Figure 1>), even the Representative Concentration Pathway (RCP hereafter) 2.6, which is often called the mild

<Figure 1> Average Temperate Projection in the Late 21$^{st}$ Century by RCP Scenarios (KMA, 2018)

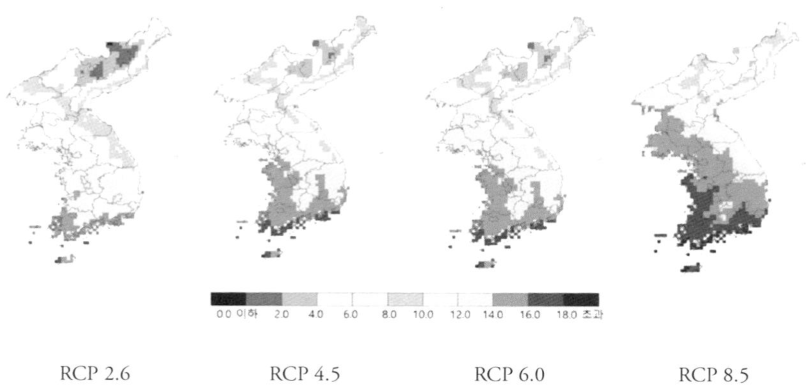

| RCP 2.6 | RCP 4.5 | RCP 6.0 | RCP 8.5 |

Source: Korea Meteorological Administration (2018)

scenario, would nevertheless lead to average temperature rise all over the Korean Peninsula. As a result, the subtropical climate zone is expected to expand to some coastal areas including the southern coast of Korean Peninsula.

In the case of the RCP 8.5 scenario, which is called the worst-case scenario, the temperature rises more rapidly, and it is predicted that a humid subtropical climate zone will be formed not only in South Korea but also in some southern parts of North Korea by the end of the 21$^{st}$ century (KMA, 2018).

Climate change along with an increase in average temperature is expected to bring about changes in many ways. The sea level rise is one of them. Since 1989, the sea level has already risen in all three seas around the Korean Peninsula. The height of increase so far has been 2.48mm in the West Sea, 3.56mm in the East Sea, and 2.44mm in the South Sea. Jeju Island, located in the southern part of the Korean Peninsula, showed an average annual sea level rise of 4.26mm. According to the forecast of sea level rise, the sea level around the Korean Peninsula will rise to 48.1cm by 2100 in RCP 4.5 and 65cm rise in the case of RCP 8.5. This consequently increases the risk of flood and inundation on the low lying areas in the coast (Heo et al., 2018).

Precipitation is another area of change. As for precipitation, a trend of greater instability can be found. Both South and North Koreas are projected to experience changes in precipitation patterns (<Figure 2>).

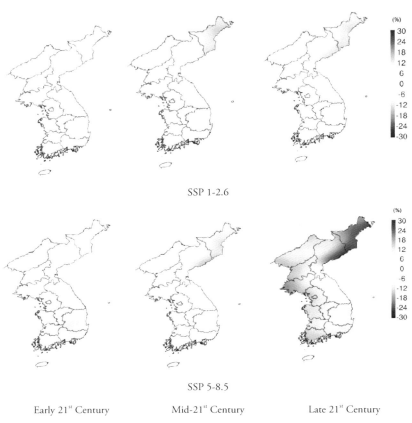

SSP 1-2.6

SSP 5-8.5

Early 21st Century          Mid-21st Century          Late 21st Century

Source: National Institute of Meteological Sciences (2020)

Temperature rise is the third area of change, as the climate change on the Korean Peninsula is progressing faster than global climate change, especially so in North Korea. The Bureau of Meteorology and Hydrology of North Korea reported in 2003 that the average annual temperature in North Korea has risen by 1.9°C over the past 100 years (Myeong et al. 2013). Seasonal changes are taking place due to overall warming, with a decrease in length by 20 days in winter and an increase by 15 days in spring and summer. This is also confirmed in the climate change analysis of the Korean Peninsula. The meteorological data for two 30-year periods, that is, 1912-1941 and 1988-2017, clearly show the seasonal changes (DPRK 2012, Korea Meteorological Administration 2012, 2018, Myeong et al. 2013)

In the case of the average annual maximum temperature, it was analyzed that South Pyongan Province, North Pyongan Province, Pyongyang City, South Hamgyong Province, and North Hamgyong Province rose relatively significantly in the RCP 2.6 scenario, and North Pyongan Province and North Hamgyong Province were analyzed to have increased relatively high. In the average annual minimum temperature, it rises a lot in South Hamgyong Province in the RCP 2.6 scenario, and in Jagang, Yanggang, and North Hamgyong Provinces in the RCP 8.5 scenario. In the case of annual precipitation, in the RCP 2.6 scenario, North Hamgyeong Province and Jagang Province increased more than other regions, and in the RCP 8.5 scenario, North Pyongan Province and North Hamgyong Province increased.

The average annual relative humidity and average wind speed were analyzed to vary depending on the region, confirming the need to respond in consideration of the climate change characteristics of the region.

## III. Climate Change Impacts on North Korea

North Korea appears to be negatively affected by climate change (DPRK, 2021, Myeong et al., 2021, 2013). The impacts of climate change are seen in many areas. For example, mean temperature rise, natural disasters, water resource shortage, coastal area damages, ecosystem change, agricultural problems, and public health problems are some areas of such impacts. Some of the these impacts will be discussed here.

Climate change can cause disruptions to agricultural production due to an increase in average temperature, which can exacerbate the food crisis. According to Dill et al. (2021), as climate change accelerates, it is highly likely that it will become difficult to grow rice and maize, the main foodstuffs in North Korea. The production of crops or fruits may become difficult in areas where they used to be grown. These effects could lead to serious food shortages, which could lead to greater difficulties for North Koreans. According to a survey on the impact of climate change on North Korea, frequent flooding and increased drought damage have negatively affected agricultural productivity (Myeong et al. 2012, 2013).

The warming caused by climate change is also changing ecosystems and areas suitable for growing crops and fruit trees. Besides, the lengthening of the days for spring and summer days makes it difficult to grow agricultural products as before. Due to climate change, the growth limit of vegetation and major crops are moving northward. According to the National Academy of Horticultural and Herbal Sciences, Rural Development Administration, the areas where fruit trees can be grown are moving northward. For example, the cultivation area for apples is expected to move northward from Daegu to Pocheon, green tea from Boseong to Goseong, tangerines from Jeju to Gimje, and peaches from Cheongdo to Paju. This means that fruit trees and crops that have been difficult to cultivate in North Korea are gradually becoming possible to grow.

Another area of the impact is the increase of pests and diseases in the forest. The forest is the main ecosystem in North Korea, and it is becoming seriously weak because of the deforestation, diseases and pests in the forest. The pests also damage the crops.

In the case of water resources, available water resources are decreasing and water quality is deteriorating. In particular, damages such as floods, droughts, and landslides are increasing. The changes in water resources have a negative impact on crop production.

Another area of damage is taking place in the structure of the ecosystem. It is said that changes are occurring not only in habitat damage but also in the biological population. In addition, the incidence of heat stroke increases during summer, which can lead to difficulty in outdoor activities.

In coastal areas, coastal erosion and salt water intrusion occur, along with increased flood damage. It is reported that climate change affects the occurrence of infectious diseases in the costal areas too.

The following table summarizes the impact of climate change in North Korea based on related literature and interviews with North Korean defectors (Myeong et al., 2021, 2013) (<Table 1>).

Table 1

**<Table 1> Impacts of Climate Change by Sector in North Korea**

| Sector | Impacts |
|---|---|
| Warming | • Overall, climate patterns are different from before<br>• Winter is getting shorter, snowfall has decreased, and spring is coming sooner.<br>• Long summer months and frequent extreme heat waves |
| Disaster | • The degree of damage and the range of damage caused by various natural disasters increase<br>• Increased frequency and intensity of floods and droughts |
| Water Resources | • Reduced availability of water resources<br>• Deterioration of water quality |
| Coastal Area | • Increase in floods in coastal areas<br>• Shoreline retreat<br>• Salt water intrusion |
| Ecosystem | • Changes in the composition of ecosystems, changes in the structure of biological communities, and changes in the number of species<br>• Changes in migration timing of animals such as migratory birds<br>• Loss of habitat<br>• Increased forest pest damage<br>• Increased wildfire damage |
| Agriculture | • Changes in crop cultivation area<br>• Change in crop growing period<br>• Reduced crop productivity, increased damage from harmful pests |
| Public health | • Increased incidences of infectious diseases<br>• Waterborne infectious diseases increase |

The fact that climate change has many impacts on North Korea is confirmed by interviews with North Korean defectors. According to an interview with defectors, North Korea is experiencing higher intensity natural disasters such as summer heat waves, floods, landslides, and drought. The climate change also causes many difficulties related to decreases in grain production and catching of fish.

## IV. Implications for Inter-Korean Cooperation on Climate Change Response

So far, the current status, prospects and impacts of climate change in North Korea have been reviewed. Since changes in the ecosystem mean changes in the habitats of endangered species or wild animals, the northward movement of habitats of endangered species in particular means that inter-Korean cooperation is required in terms of ecosystem management and biological resources. In addition, changes in agricultural fields are directly related to food, indicating that inter-Korean cooperation is necessary in the agricultural sector to maintain the existing diet in the future. As concerns about not only the ecosystem but also infectious diseases have recently increased, cooperation on vector-borne diseases that are closely related to climate change is necessary. The increase in frequency and intensity of natural disasters causes great damage not only to human life and property, but also to society as a whole. North Korea has suffered enormous damages from extreme floods and droughts since the late 1990s.

Therefore, cooperation to strengthen the capacity to respond to natural disasters is also necessary. The drought or extreme cold waves can be solved by supplying water resources-related infrastructure and heating energy. Cooperation for the expansion of such infrastructure is necessary to reduce the damage caused by climate change in North Korea.

In the United Nations Framework Convention on Climate Change, the Paris Agreement has been signed in which all parties participate in greenhouse gas reduction efforts to mitigate climate change. AThe international community has submitted a voluntary reduction plan, and recently, including South Korea, the world is declaring carbon neutrality.

North Korea also submitted an INDC as a party to the treaty. In 2016, the country submitted the INDC to the United Nations Framework Convention on Climate Change in which the country announced that it would voluntarily reduce 8% of its total emissions, and with the support of the international community, reduce it by 32.25% additionally, which corresponds to 40.25% of the country's total emissions (<Figure 3>).

<Figure 3> North Korea's Total Emissions and Its Plan to Reduce the Emission

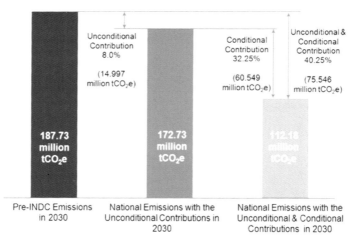

Source: NDRK(2016)

In the 2nd NDC submitted in 2019, North Korea presented a greenhouse gas reduction target that was 16.4% higher than the INDC submitted in 2016. North Korea declared that it would actively participate in the international community's efforts to reduce greenhouse gases. This means that North Korea is willing to participate in global efforts to solve the climate change problem. Then it will be possible to contribute to carbon neutrality by promoting inter-Korean cooperation. More than anything else, cooperation in the dimension of adaptation to climate change in consideration of the impact and vulnerability of North Korea's climate change needs to be prioritized, and cooperation in the dimension of mitigation of climate change through greenhouse gas reduction needs to be promoted together.

In 2016, North Korea presented a list of potential areas that would contribute to mitigate climate change. As seen at <Table 2>, the list indicates that energy and heating sectors are what North Korea is eager the most to modernize. In particular, the house heating and construction are included in North Korea's hopeful priorities for international cooperation. North Korea also seems to want to enhance its management of the environment. South Korea could consider advancing cooperative projects with North Korea in those fields. Other topics, such as agriculture, sanitation, water resource control, and preservation of ecosystems, would be potential areas where inter-Korean cooperation could be materialized.

<Table 2> The DPRK's Priority List for International Support in Its First NDC (DPRK, 2016)

| No | Mitigation Measures Prioritized for Conditional Contribution |
|----|---------------------------------------------------------------|
| 1 | To reduce power transmission and distribution losses to 6% |
| 2 | To build 2 000MW nuclear power station |
| 3 | To install a total of 1 000MW grid connected solar PV systems |
| 4 | To build a total of 500MW West Sea off–shore wind farms at the Korean West Sea |
| 5 | To build a total of 500MW on-shore wind farms |
| 6 | To use energy-efficient air conditioners and heat pumps instead of coal-fired space heating at households and offices |
| 7 | To use biogas from livestock manure and domestic sewage instead of coal or firewood for cooking |
| 8 | To replace coal use for hot water with solar hot water system at households |
| 9 | To replace conventional wood stoves for cooking with efficient wood stoves at rural households |
| 10 | To build the rice husk cogeneration plants |
| 11 | To building centralized compositing facilities to collect and treat municipal solid waste |
| 12 | To replace the old subcritical coal power stations with ultra-supercritical coal power stations |
| 13 | To increase additives (blast furnace slag or fly ash) from 15% to 50% in blended cement |
| 14 | To build biogas plants treating municipal solid waste |
| 15 | To replace conventional coal stoves for cooking with efficient electric cookers at the households |
| 16 | To reduce 25% of energy consumption in industry through technical modernization by 2030 |
| 17 | To replace tunnel brick kilns with vertical shaft brick kilns |
| 18 | To introduce the Bus Rapid Transit systems in large cities |
| 19 | To scale up agroforestry and sustainable forest management |

Source: NDRK(2016)

The shared concern on global climate change between the two Koreas could actually come to fruition on the basis of the inter-Korean agreement, that is, the Pyongyang Declaration in 2018. Announced during the 3rd inter-Korean summit held in Pyongyang, the North Korea's capital, the agreement made by the two Koreas' leaders contains an article that articulates their commitment that two Koreas would pursue environmental cooperation for preservation and restoration of natural ecosystem. In particular, restoration of forest ecosystem will be of priority in the inter-Korean cooperation, which should bring about the substantive outcome. South and North Koreas will be able to seek to cooperate in addressing the climate change once circumstances become favorable.


## V. Conclusion

Inter-Korean cooperation requires cooperation between the South and North Koreas to respond to climate change, and it is beneficial to both Koreas. In addition, environmental cooperation will help them to build mutual trust, contributing to the establishment of peace on the Korean Peninsula. The followings are proposed for effective inter-Korean cooperation. First, cooperation in which synergies can be derived should be promoted in consideration of both mitigation of and adaptation to climate change. Second, extremely vulnerable areas, such as agriculture, ecosystem, and water resources, should be prioritized for cooperation. Third, inter-Korean cooperation to respond to climate change should serve as an opportunity to restore natural ecosystems. The United Nations has declared the decade of ecosystem restoration for 2021-2030. It will be advantageous to cooperate with the international community as it responds to climate change and at the same time participates in international efforts to restore the damaged ecosystem on the Korean Peninsula. Fourth, it is necessary to proceed with the infrastructure that can prevent and mitigate floods, droughts, and other natural disasters. Fifth, inter-Korean cooperation to achieve the UN's SDGs should be achieved. Inter-Korean cooperation to respond to climate change will greatly help to achieve carbon neutrality and net zero not only on the Korean Peninsula but also in the world.

# Cooperation between South and North Koreas for net-zero emissions on the Korean Peninsula with NBS & REDD+

## I. Introduction

It is obvious that people's focus has already shifted from whether or not carbon neutrality is important to how we can reach carbon neutrality. Since the establishment of United Nations Framework Convention on Climate Change (UNFCCC) in 1992, countries around the world have exerted efforts to cooperate together to resolve the worldwide issue (Rogelj at al. 2015a, 2015b, van de Ven et al. 2021; van Soest et al. 2021; Moghaddasi et al. 2021). Currently, the temperature of the earth has risen by 1.1°C compared to the pre-industrial era (1850-1900). Should Greenhouse Gas (GHG) emission continue at the present pace, the global temperature increase would become 1.5°C by 2040 (IPCC AR6, 2021; Su, 2017). Judging from the recent emergence of powerful floods and wildfires, which we are witnessing in the past couple of years, we can expect that the 1.5°C rise of temperature might cause several times stronger natural disasters than the previous ones (Cheung et al., 2016; Tanaka and O'Neill, 2018; IPCC AR6, 2021). A study published by World Wide Fund for Nature (WWF) predicts that with 1.5°C temperature increase would bring about 0.3-0.93m sea level rise, affecting 46 million people across the world, as well as the unimaginable event of the total melting of the Artic Sea, which would happen once every 100 years (Finlayson, 2018).

In order to minimize carbon emissions, South Korea has already announced "the 2050 carbon neutrality plan." In a strict sense, carbon neutrality is different from the concept of Net-zero or Climate Neutral, which can be accomplished by the zero emission of GHG. On the other hand, carbon neutrality concerns the emission of $CO_2$ although the slogan of "carbon neutrality" is accepted by South Koreans as the same meaning as Net-zero or Climate Neutral.

It cannot be emphasized enough that reaching carbon neutrality means the control of both emission and absorption. In other words, we should find ways to minimize the emissions while seeking to maximize the absorption of $CO_2$ from the atmosphere. From that perspective, as crucial and plausible tool to achieve carbon neutrality, the so-called Nature Based Solution (NBS) and Reducing Emissions from Deforestation and forest Degradation (REDD+) have recently drawn attention.

Because environmental issues of the Korean Peninsula cannot be solved by efforts of either South or North Korea alone, cooperation between the two Koreas must be attempted. One of such areas that may permit the inter-Korean cooperation without violating the sanctions is making mutual effort to preserve forests, which are also necessary to reach carbon neutrality in the Korean Peninsula. This paper will address the importance of NBS and REDD+ in the Korean peninsula and examine the prospect of cooperation between the two Koreas with particular focus on the forests and the land of the Korean Peninsula.

## II. Importance of NBS and REDD+ as Key Concepts for Carbon Neutrality

The preservation of forests and the issues of global warming are closely intertwined. As we lose more and more areas of forest with natural disasters, such as recent wildfires in California and floods in China, as well as artificial deforestation as can be seen in the Amazon Rainforest, the global warming will accelerate. If humankind maintains current level of greenhouse gas emissions, it is very likely that the global temperature will rise by 1.5°C by 2040 though it has already risen by 1.1°C thus far. If the global temperature rose by 1.5 °C, such natural disasters and extreme climate events, as flood, drought, hurricane, typhoon, and wildfire, could be expected to happen with more frequency and intensity, which will lead to more loss of forests and consequently deteriorate the trend of global warming. If the temperature rise should reach 2°C, more terrifying results will take place: the ice in the

Artic Sea will melt once every ten years, while 99% of the coral reefs will go extinct.

In order to prevent the deteriorating global warming, it is necessary to not just reach carbon neutrality but also achieve the net zero, which means the zero emission of greenhouse gas (GHG), including not only carbon dioxide ($CO_2$) but also other materials like methane ($CH_4$), nitrous oxide ($N_2O$), Hydrofluorocarbons (HFCs), Perfluorocarbons (PFCs), Sulfur hexafluoride ($SF_6$), Nitrogen trifluoride ($NF_3$) and so on.

As well demonstrated by the unprecedented level of frequency and severity of natural disasters, the global warming has been posing crises all around the world, which everyone of human kind must cooperate to address. One of important parts of such efforts should be carbon absorption. Regarding the methods for absorbing $CO_2$ from the atmosphere, NBS, CCUS, and DAC are counted.

The nature-based solutions (NBS) refer to actions that sustainably protect, manage, and restore natural or modified ecosystems. It is a way to use nature in order to address various environmental challenges. The types of NBS are numerous: forest, prairie, urban wetland, urban forest, coastal wetlands, inland wetlands, low areas where inundation and flooding happen, mangroves, and all other green spaces can be the places that NBS is applied. The NBS approach has recently drawn attention and begun to be widely discussed by experts as recommended way of carbon absorption by Intergovernmental Panel on Climate Change (IPCC), International Union for Conservation of Nature (IUCN), and the European Union (EU) (Cohen-Shacham et al., 2016; Li, 2018).

Since NBS pursues the sustainable management and use of nature for solving various environmental problems, there might be questions about its effectiveness. To the surprise of many, more and more evidence is being found that NBS proves effective and has enormous potential to address socio environmental challenges. While NBS will serve as the main repository of storing $CO_2$, it has different ecological functions for addressing water shortage, water pollution, food ecurity, human health biodiversity, and disaster risk management (Kabisch, 2016; Faivre, 2017).

NBS has been compared to other methods of reducing $CO_2$. For example, the Carbon Capture, Usage and Storage (CCUS), which targets emission from power plants, is regarded as an important way due to its high capacity in capturing a large amount of $CO_2$. Thus, an increasing amount of investment are being made for research and development of CCUS. However, there are disadvantages of CCUS. CCUS facilities would be expensive to build and manage, consuming considerable resources and energy. It is also difficult to find locations for CCUS because of the possibility of leaking the stored $CO_2$ with unexpected events, such as earthquakes. Therefore, given advantages, it is almost impossible for human kind to rely solely on CCUS methods.

Another option that we may consider taking to reduce $CO_2$ is the device called Direct Air Capture (DAC). DAC is designed to capture $CO_2$ directly from the air by using filters or chemical materials. The method has already been widely accepted around world. For example, the largest DAC facility in the world built in Iceland is known to have the capability of capturing

40 million ton of $CO_2$ per year. The artificial tree with DAC technology, which was established in Mexico, could capture 368 times as much $CO_2$ as a natural tree. This method is drawing attention from world leaders like Bill Gates, who has made a good deal of investment. Nevertheless, since the level of DAC technology still remains to be developed, there are still uncertainties in the future for DAC to function with full capability. If it should cost a lot of money, energy, or water to operate the DAC facilities, it cannot be an appropriate method to reduce $CO_2$. In general, it is expected to cost about $600 to $1,000 to capture 1 ton of $CO_2$ using DAC. In fact, in order for this technology to become more widely available and commercial, it would be necessary for scientists to find a way of lowering the cost down below $100 per ton of $CO_2$. Therefore, in comparison with CCUS or DAC, NBS has clear advantages in cost-effectiveness and energy efficiency, being the far safer and easier way to decrease $CO_2$ level in the air.

Along with NBS, REDD+ is recognized to be one of the most important concepts. The concept of REDD was suggested by the United Nations Framework Convention on Climate Change (UNFCCC) in 2005. Two years later, a critical addition was made to the concept, which emphasizes conservation, sustainable management of forests and enhancement of forest carbon stocks in developing countries, hence turning REDD into REDD+. The idea essentially calls on developed countries to help developing countries develop with Sustainable Development Goals (SDGs). In other words, to prevent deforestation and forest degradation, all the countries should work together for developing countries to address such economic and environmental issues as agricultural expansion, excessive livestock farming, forest biomass and wildfire. The management of REDD+ includes a multiple sets of projects administered by different institutions under UN, such as measurement, reporting, and verification (MRV) by Food and Agriculture Organization (FAO), national REDD+ governance by United Nations Development Programme (UNDP), ensuring multiple benefits of forests and REDD+ by United Nations Environment Programme (UNEP); transparent, equitable, and accountable management of REDD+ payments by UNDP; and REDD+ as a catalyst for transformations to a green economy by UNEP.

With all the concepts in mind, the following part of this paper is devoted to discussion on the potentials of NBS and REDD+ for our efforts to achieve carbon neutrality.

## III. Forests as Key Carbon Sink

Notwithstanding the ideal of complete prevention of carbon emission, one cannot just focus on the environment without considering economy. Governments around world have been struggling to achieve the two seemingly opposite goals. In that context, the concept of maximizing the carbon absorption comes to forward. As mentioned above, reaching carbon neutrality necessitate the control of both the carbon source and the carbon absorption. Here comes the new concept, the "carbon sink." The carbon sink refers to any reservoirs to absorb $CO_2$ from the atmosphere.

The aforementioned three methods of carbon absorption, namely NBS, CCUS and DAC, have been recognized as crucial categories of the carbon sink to achieve the goal of net zero. Nevertheless, due to the involved side-effects of CCUS and DAS as we examined above, the ideal picture of carbon absorption at the moment should be the maximum use of NBS but the minimum use of DAC and CCUS.

Among the various ways of NBS, the forestation was of crucial importance especially at this moment. The forest is one of the most effective means of absorbing carbon relative to the cost. Building forests offers ecological benefits that help us create an environment where the human beings and other organisms can coexist in harmony. On the other hand, forest degradation, which has occurred in the various places of the world for natural and economic reasons, does not just lead to reduction in carbon absorption but also tends to cause other damages. The burning of forests creates more emission, exacerbating climate change. Forest degradation is almost always coupled with soil degradation. Flooding and landslide, which are often accompanied by sedimentation and land pollution, are other major effects of forest degradation. Furthermore, the degraded forests are also very difficult to restore, which would take 80-100 years naturally or 30-40 years through artificial forestation.

The problem is that the recent trend of global warming creates a sort of vicious circle of forest degradation. The wildfire in regions like California is happening becoming more frequent and more severe, devastating increasing areas of forest. Then, with less capability of absorbing $CO_2$, the global warming intensifies, which leads to more wildfire and other natural disasters that would destroy more forests.

As for forest degradation's effect on soil degradation, it is necessary to consider the soil's benefit to contain $CO_2$. One of the topics discussed at the 21st UNFCCC COP21 was about the role of soil as represented by the slogan "4 per mille soils for food security and climate." Here the choice of the number of 0.4% can be explained by the fact that the annual carbon emission of 8.9 giga tons (Gt) can be offset by the 0.4 % of soil storage (2,400 Gt) of carbon. Therefore, it should be emphasized that soil plays crucial role in containing carbon and thus reducing carbon in the atmosphere. (Minasny et al., 2017) In South Korea alone, the annual loss of soil amounts to over 341 million tons, which means that the value of 22 million dollars of carbon is lost from soil every year. Apart from carbon, other minerals like nitrogen or phosphorus are being lost, causing million dollars to be wasted in vain through soil degradation (Jang et al., 2021).

## IV. Reforestation in South Korea

South Korea has made efforts to create and maintain its forests since the 1950s. During the Japanese colonial period (1910-1945) and around the Korean War (1950-1953), forests had been destroyed not just by the Japanese colonial policy aftermath of wars but also by people who needed fuel. As 80 percent of the fuels used in households were firewood, even the trees in the deepest of the mountains were logged down. The UN report published in 1969 claimed that the forest degradation in South Korea was "chronic" and "uncurable." However, after finding a balance in energy sources, coupled with the aid from the international community, South Korea was able to recover forests. It is widely accepted that South Koreans had planted about 10 billion trees between 1973 and 1987. The result was remarkable. The area of forests in South Korea amounts to 6.3 million hectares, which comprises 62.6% of the entire land territory. Recently, as economic development intensifies, however, thousands of hectares of forests began to disappear every year.

According to the carbon neutrality scenario planned by South Korea's 2050 Carbon Neutrality Committee, the carbon absorption target is set to absorb 25.3 million tons by using NBS, 84.6 million tons by CCUS, and 7.4 million tons by DAC. Here the large part of the NBS goal is supposed to be covered by forests. However, as reflected by the rearrangement of the target carbon absorption by NBS from 41.3 million tons in 2018 to 25.3 million tons in 2050, the loss of forests seems accelerating.

In terms of carbon absorption ability of trees, another problem that South Korea has in its management of forests is the lowering capability of trees to absorb $CO_2$ as they grow older. Therefore, it is necessary to consider continual planting of young trees although we need more information and research for better understanding of the relationship between the age of the trees as well as their absorption capacity.

## V. Inter-Korean Cooperation for Forestation

Given the aforementioned importance of the forest in the Korean Peninsula, it will be crucial for South Korea and North Korea to cooperate together. It seems that there is a sort of consensus between the two Korean governments as well as experts regarding the great potential that cooperation in forestation would bring. Needless to say, South Korea, aiming at reducing GHG, needs to secure a carbon sink, while North Korea wants to prevent natural disasters that have become more frequent and serious than ever before. Thus, the cooperation in building forests will be a great win-win model for both parties.

When it comes to the situation in North Korea, due to the ongoing economic crisis, North Korea has been experiencing persistent forest degradation, which is becoming worse as time goes by. North Koreans have taken advantage of the forests for fire woods. In addition, many of them still stick to slash-and-burn farming, which have led to an enormous loss of forests. Floods and landslides, which take place more often than before, also quicken the process of land degradations in North Korea. According to data, the total area of forests in North Korea was about 8.2 million hectares in 1990, then it shrunk to be about 6.24 million hectares in 2010 and about 6 million hectares in 2020.

Despite the economic difficulties, North Korea has proclaimed a commitment to achieve carbon neutrality. The representatives of the DPRK actually participated in a meeting of parties for the international convention on the environment and expressed the country's will to take part in the global effort to protect the environment. As a follow-up measure, the DPRK has established a sustainable development national task force as well. North Kore also published its Voluntary National Reviews (VNR) report, where it has actually revised its greenhouse gas reduction target. The report in 2021, compared to the 2018, did revise up the target. North Korea's target was set to reduce GHG by 50.34% although the target could be accomplished on the condition that it received aid from abroad. At any rate, the report shows that North Korea wants assistance from the international community.

Then, how two Koreas could cooperate for carbon neutrality? First and foremost, the two Koreas share the same experience of forest degradation, whereas only South Korea could overcome it. South Korea turned the tide as it achieved economic growth and reforestation at the same time. In that context, South Korea can be helpful to North Korea because the former knows what the latter is going through and how to solve the problems. If South Korea could help North Korea restore the loss of forests that occurred between 1990 to 2020, which is 2.2 million hectares, the total amount of carbon absorption would increase by 1.7 million to 2.2 million tons.

The forestation in North Korea would be achieved not just by planting trees. It requires energy supply that will help North Korean people transform their energy sources without depending on firewood for energy source. South Korea has enough technology and resources for North Korea to improve the basic energy infrastructure with. It is reported that North Korea suffers as much as 50 percent of transmission and distribution loss due to the aged power generation infrastructure. In this process, the two Korean may consider adopting renewable energy supply as an auxiliary source of power. North Korea has more favorable condition than South for the renewable energy generation with more sunlight and wind. The DPRK is estimated to have the potential of 1502 Terawatt-hour (TWh) for solar power and 1130 TWh for wind compared to South Korea's 411 TWh and 942 TWh each. In addition, smart grid systems set by the village, equipped with Energy Storage System (ESS)s, would be helpful for reducing the transmission and distribution loss because it will greatly enhance effectiveness with manageable systems along with relative short distance from power sources.

The expected outcome of inter-Korean cooperation based on REDD+ is very promising. Only with NBS, the two Koreas would be able to secure an additional carbon absorption of approximately 5 million tons by 2050, which would cover around 20% of the total carbon emission in the Korean Peninsula. If CCUS and DAC would follow, the amount of carbon absorption will increase to approximately 14 million tons. Of course, more systemic cooperation would bring in more positive results.

In order to successfully implement this effort, both South and North Korea do need international cooperation. Both Koreas should draw worldwide attention to the issue. Once the two Koreas make it a global agenda, they will be able to win not only assistance and funding from the international community but also permission and support that would allow two Koreas to work together without worrying about the sanctions against North Korea.

As a matter of fact, North Korea's forest and land degradation is an international challenge that might slower the global effort toward carbon neutrality. As a global issue pertaining to the international environment, forest degradation in North Korea will garner the attention of the global community. North Korea's problems regarding its shortage of water, food, and energy, the direct results of its forest degradation, concern UN SDGs. Furthermore, soil degradation accompanied by forest degradation is related to United Nations Convention to Combat Desertification (UNCCD) as well.

Probably recognizing the significance of restoring North Korea's forest and soil, a number of international organizations have attempted to carry out various projects. For example, Hanns Seidel Foundation, a German international organization, carried out a series of projects for forestation and preservation of wetlands in North Korea between 2015 and 2017. Other international organizations, such as Green Climate Fund (GCF), Global Environment Facility (GEF), and UNEP, seek to cooperate with North Korea. The initiatives taken by those international community would make it possible for the two Koreas to work together to address environmental issues, including forestation and preventing land degradation.

One possible way to actualize inter-Korean cooperation might be South Korea's support on North Korea's flood control. As North Korea's Rodong Daily Newspaper admits, flood in North Korea poses serious threats to North Korea's food security. World Food Programme (WFP) warns that North Korea will suffer from food shortage that amounts to 860 thousand tons, which is caused by floods. North Korea's unstable food supply seems not to be easily resoluble because experts predict that 63% of the entire population of North Korea will be under the thread of food shortage until 2031. If North Korea is willing to accept South Korea's help for preventing floods, there are many parts that two Koreas could cooperate in: they can work together to build an early warning system, improve infrastructure, particularly sewerage and other water management system, restore forests, and modernize the grid system etc. If the cooperation is accomplished, South Korea could achieve the carbon neutrality, and North Korea could improve their disaster control capability.

In conclusion, as the notion of the carbon sink and the importance of carbon absorption come forward, the cooperation in forestation and stopping forest degradation in the Korean Peninsula draws attention. As a representative case of REDD+, the successful inter-Korean environmental cooperation will benefit the two Koreas in various ways. Both of them can solve economic and environmental problems, such as carbon neutrality and flood prevention. The two Koreas will have better national images, and the experience of cooperation itself will contribute to the establishment of a peace regime on the Korean Peninsula.

## Part 1. The Border Wall on the Korean Peninsula in Global Context

_____ Reece Jones

1    https://legal.un.org/repertory/art2.shtml


## Part 3. Environmental Agenda and Practice of Using ESG Criteria in Russia

_____ Sergey Lukonin

1    http://www.kremlin.ru/acts/bank/7188

2    https://www.mid.ru/ru/foreign_policy/news/1653295/

3    https://www.garant.ru/products/ipo/prime/doc/72661694/

4    http://www.kremlin.ru/supplement/5731

5    https://docs.cntd.ru/document/560982425

6    https://docs.cntd.ru/document/499073502

7    https://docs.cntd.ru/document/901725097

8    https://www.mnr.gov.ru/activity/international_agreements/

9    http://www.consultant.ru/document/cons_doc_LAW_34823/

10    http://www.consultant.ru/document/cons_doc_LAW_22971/

11    http://www.consultant.ru/document/cons_doc_LAW_19109/

12    http://www.consultant.ru/document/cons_doc_LAW_8515/

13    http://www.consultant.ru/document/cons_doc_LAW_6072/

14    https://www.mnr.gov.ru/docs/strategii_i_doktriny/142854/

15    http://static.government.ru/media/files/ADKkCzp3fWO32e2yA0BhtIpyzWfHaiUa.pdf

16    http://static.government.ru/media/files/ADKkCzp3fWO32e2yA0BhtIpyzWfHaiUa.pdf

17    http://min.prirodyair.tilda.ws

18    https://ecologyofrussia.ru/proekt/vnedrenie-nailuchshih-dostupnyh-tehnologij/

19    https://tass.ru/ekonomika/5598685

20    https://old.economy.gov.ru/minec/about/structure/depGostarif/2016191101

21  http://www.cenef.ru/file/Bashmakov_14.pdf

22  https://www.economy.gov.ru/material/news/rossiya_soobshchila_o_svoem_pervom_opredelyaemom_na_nacionalnom_urovne_vklade_v_realizaciyu_parizhskogo_soglasheniya.html

23  https://ac.gov.ru/uploads/2-Publications/BRE/_октябрь_web.pdf

24  https://ecfor.ru/wp-content/uploads/2017/05/fedorov-rossijskij-uglerodnyj-balans.pdf

25  https://unfccc.int/sites/default/files/resource/10469275_Russian%20Federation-BR4-1-4BR_RUS.pdf

26  https://www.kommersant.ru/doc/5183510

27  https://www.kommersant.ru/doc/5041024

28  https://cceis.hse.ru/data/2021/04/13/1391067174/doklad_povorot-k-prirode.pdf

29  https://cceis.hse.ru/data/2021/04/13/1391067174/doklad_povorot-k-prirode.pdf

30  https://cceis.hse.ru/data/2021/04/13/1391067174/doklad_povorot-k-prirode.pdf

31  https://news.rambler.ru/community/47352872-nazvany-samye-gryaznye-goroda-rossii/

32  https://www.forbes.ru/obshchestvo-photogallery/402193-krupneyshaya-katastrofa-v-arktike-chto-izvestno-o-razlive-topliva

33  https://www.kommersant.ru/doc/4366214?query=пясино

34  http://government.ru/news/43297/

35  https://sozd.duma.gov.ru/bill/37939-8

36  https://www2.deloitte.com/ru/ru/pages/about-deloitte/press-releases/2021/esg-banking.html

37  https://www.kommersant.ru/doc/4704049

38  https://sistema.ru/press/pressreleases/afk-sistema-vpervye-privlekaet-esg-finansirovanie-v-sberbanke-

39  https://mkb.ru/news/40241

40  https://sovcombank.ru/articles/novosti-kompanii/sovkombank-privlek-sinditsirovannii-kredit-350-mln-s-esg-transhem-na-finansirovanie-kart-halva

41  https://www.kommersant.ru/doc/4713497

42  https://www.kommersant.ru/doc/4713497

43  https://raexpert.eu/esg_corporate_ranking/

44  https://www.banki.ru/news/lenta/?id=10942068

45  https://www.kommersant.ru/doc/4713497

46  https://www.vedomosti.ru/press_releases/2021/04/22/rusal-nachal-testovie-postavki-alyuminiya-s-samim-nizkim-v-mire-uglerodnim-sledom

47  https://blackterminal.com/articles/esg-v-rossii-lidery-ustojcivogo-razvitia-i-psevdozelen

iteli?hl=ru

48   https://blackterminal.com/articles/esg-v-rossii-lidery-ustojcivogo-razvitia-i-psevdozelenite
li?hl=ru

## Part 4.  From Green Growth to Green Diplomacy:
## Japanese Domestic and International Initiatives Towards
## a Carbon Neutral Society _____ Sebastian Maslow

1   Prime Minister of Japan and His Cabinet, "COP26 World Leaders Summit Statement by
Prime Minister Kishida Fumio," November 2, 2021, https://japan.kantei.go.jp/100_kishida/
statement/202111/_00002.html.

2   Julie Gilson, "From Kyoto to Glasgow: Is Japan a Climate Leader?" *Pacific Review*, DOI:
10.1080/09512748.2021.2008475.

3   Toshio Kawada, Keisuke Katori, and Junichiro Nagasaki, "Japan won't sign COP26 statement
on ending use of coal-fired plants," *The Asahi Shimbun* (November 5, 2021), https://www.
asahi.com/ajw/articles/14475626. Unless otherwise stated, all online sources were accessed and
available on February 16, 2022.

4   Junichiro Nagasaki, "Japan OKs plan to double use of renewables for energy by 2030," *The
Asahi Shimbun* (October 22, 2021), https://www.asahi.com/ajw/articles/14466293.

5   For earlier work on Japan's climate diplomacy see Miranda A. Schreurs, *Environmental
Politics in Japan, Germany, and the United States* (Cambridge: Cambridge University Press,
2003); Yasuko Kameyama, *Climate Change Policy in Japan: From the 1980s to 2015* (London:
Routledge, 2016).

6   Chalmers Johnson, *MITI and the Japanese Miracle: The Growth of Industrial Policy, 1925-
1975* (Stanford, CA: Stanford University Press, 1982); Richard J. Samuels, *The Business of the
Japanese State: Energy Markets in Comparative and Historical Perspective* (Ithaca, NJ: Cornell
University Press, 1987); Jeffrey Broadbent, *Environmental Politics in Japan* (Cambridge:
Cambridge University Press, 1998).

7   Llewelyn Hughes, "Energy Policy in Japan: Revisiting Radical Incrementalism," in *The Oxford
Handbook of Japanese Politics*, ed. Robert J. Pekkanen and Saadia M. Pekkanen (Oxford:
Oxford University Press, 2022), 377-394.

8   For details of this initiative see https://www.mofa.go.jp/mofaj/gaiko/kankyo/kiko/coolearth50/
index.html.

9   Prime Minister of Japan and His Cabinet, "Action Plan for Achieving a Low-carbon Society,"

July 29, 2008, https://japan.kantei.go.jp/policy/ondanka/final080729.pdf.

10    John S. Duffield and Brian Woodall, "Japan's New Basic Energy Plan," *Energy Policy* 39, no. 6 (2011): 3741–3749.

11    Joshua Meltzer, "After Fukushima: What's Next for Japan's Energy and Climate Change Policy," Global Economy and Development (Brookings Institution, September 7, 2011).

12    Eri Sugiura and Akane Okutsu, "Why Japan finds coal hard to quit," *Nikkei Asia* (November 21, 2018), https://asia.nikkei.com/Spotlight/The-Big-Story/Why-Japan-finds-coal-hard-to-quit.

13    Richard J. Samuels, *3.11: Disaster and Change in Japan* (Ithaca, NJ: Cornell University Press, 2013); Koichi Hasegawa, Beyond Fukushima: Toward a Post-Nuclear Society (Melbourne: Trans Pacific Press, 2015).

14    Iris Wieczorek, "Energy Transition in Japan: From Consensus to Controversy," GIGA Focus Asia 1 (January 2019).

15    Florentine Koppenborg, "Nuclear Restart Politics: How the 'Nuclear Village' Lost Policy Implementation Power," *Social Science Japan Journal* 24, no. 1 (2021): 115–135.

16    Christian Wirth and Sebastian Maslow, "Introduction: *Crisis Narratives, Institutional Change, and the Transformation of the Japanese State*," in Crisis Narratives, Institutional Change, and the Transformation of the Japanese State, ed. Sebastian Maslow and Christian Wirth (Albany: State University of New York Press, 2021): 1–22.

17    Prime Minister and His Cabinet, "Japan Revitalization Strategy — Japan is Back," June 14, 2013, https://www.kantei.go.jp/jp/singi/keizaisaisei/pdf/en_saikou_jpn_hon.pdf.

18    Keidanren, "A Proposal for Future Energy Policy," October 15, 2013, https://www.keidanren.or.jp/en/policy/2013/089.html.

19    For the 2014 BEP see https://www.enecho.meti.go.jp/en/category/others/basic_plan/pdf/4th_strategic_energy_plan.pdf.

20    Mainichi, "Decommissioning of troubled fast-breeder reactor Monju would cost 300 billion yen," *The Mainichi* (February 16, 2016), https://mainichi.jp/english/articles/20160216/p2a/00m/0na/005000c; Mainichi, "Decommissioning of Monju reactor would affect nuclear fuel cycle project," *The Mainichi* (September 21, 2016), https://mainichi.jp/english/articles/20160921/p2a/00m/0na/013000c.

21    For the 2018 BEP see https://www.meti.go.jp/english/press/2018/pdf/0703_002c.pdf.

22    METI, "Basic Hydrogen Strategy," https://www.meti.go.jp/english/press/2017/1226_003.html. Nikkei, "Japan to push for hydrogen society," *Nikkei Asia* (April 12, 2020), https://asia.nikkei.com/Politics/Japan-to-push-for-hydrogen-society.

23   Daniel Aldrich, Philip Y. Lipsy, and Mary M. McCarthy, "Japan's opportunity to lead," *Nature Climate Change* 9 (July 2019): 492.

24   Gregory W. Noble, "METI's Miraculous Comeback and the Uncertain Future of Japanese Industrial Policy," *The Oxford Handbook of Japanese Politics*, ed. Robert J. Pekkanen and Saadia M. Pekkanen (Oxford: Oxford University Press, 2022): 353–375.

25   Kosuke Takeuchi, "All Abe's men: Japan's economy ministry sidelined under Suga," Nikkei Asia (September 17, 2020); see also Ken Sofer, "Climate politics in Japan: The impacts of public opinion, bureaucratic rivalries, and interest groups on Japan's environmental agenda," Sasakawa USA Forum Issue no.1 (May 20, 2016), https://spfusa.org/wp-content/uploads/2016/05/Sofer-Climate-Politics-in-Japan.pdf

26   Timothy Fraser and Daniel P. Aldrich, "The Fukushima effect at home: The changing role of domestic actors in Japanese energy policy," *WIREs Climate Change* 11, no. 5 (2020), DOI: 10.1002/wcc.655; Yasuko Kameyama, "Climate Change Policy: Can New Actors Affect Japan's Policy-Making in the Paris Agreement Era," *Social Science Japan Journal* 24, no. 1 (2021): 67–84.

27   Wieczorek, "Energy Transition in Japan." The Japanese government promotes the city of Yonago as an example of a self-reliant community; see https://www.japan.go.jp/sustainable_future/innovators_unlocking_globalsolutions/03.html.

28   See Japan Climate Initiative, https://japanclimate.org.

29   Global Sustainable Investment Alliance, "2018 Global Sustainable Investment Review," http://www.gsi-alliance.org/wp-content/uploads/2019/03/GSIR_Review2018.3.28.pdf.

30   Trevor Incerti and Phillip Y. Lipsy, "The Politics of Energy and Climate Change in Japan under Abe," *Asian Survey* 58, no. 4 (2018): 607–634; Ulrich Volz, "Renewable energy: Abe's missing arrow," *East Asia Forum* (September 2, 2015), https://www.eastasiaforum.org/2015/09/02/renewable-energy-abes-missing-arrow/. For counterargument see Andrew DeWit, "Japan's Bid to Become a World Leader in Renewable Energy," *Asia-Pacific Journal* 13/40, no. 2 (October 5, 2015), https://apjjf.org/-Andrew-DeWit/4385.

31   As of 2019, Japan imports 99.7 percent of its oil, 97.5 percent of its natural gas, and 99.3 percent of its coal; see Agency for Natural Resources and Energy, "2019-Understanding the current energy situation in Japan," August 13, 2019, https://www.enecho.meti.go.jp/en/category/special/article/energyissue2019_01.html.

32   Nikkei, "Japan seeks stoppage of 100 inefficient coal plants in a decade," *Nikkei Asia* (July 2, 2020), https://asia.nikkei.com/Business/Energy/Japan-seeks-stoppage-of-100-inefficient-coal-plants-in-a-decade; Florentine Koppenborg and Ulv Hanssen, "Japan's growing

dependence on coal," *East Asia Forum* (March 22, 2020), https://www.eastasiaforum. org/2020/03/22/japans-growing-dependence-on-coal/.

33 Rintaro Sakurai, "Japan logs sharp rise in renewable energy output amid pandemic," *The Asahi Shimbun* (September 25, 2020), https://www.asahi.com/ajw/articles/13759257.

34 Nick Butler, "Suga must seize the opportunity to change Japan's energy mix," *Nikkei Asia* (October 16, 2020), https://asia.nikkei.com/Opinion/Suga-must-seize-the-opportunity-to-change-Japan-s-energy-mix.

35 Nikkei, "Suga vows to meet Japan's zero-emissions goal by 2050," *Nikkei Asia* (October 26, 2020), https://asia.nikkei.com/Politics/Suga-vows-to-meet-Japan-s-zero-emissions-goal-by-2050; Azusa Kawakami, "Suga's 2050 zero-carbon goal thrusts Japan into green tech race," *Nikkei Asia* (October 27, 2020), https://asia.nikkei.com/Spotlight/Environment/Climate-Change/Suga-s-2050-zero-carbon-goal-thrusts-Japan-into-green-tech-race; Mari Yamaguchi, "Post-Abe agenda: Suga says Japan to carbon-free by 2050," *AP News* (October 26, 2020), https://apnews.com/article/virus-outbreak-shinzo-abe-cabinets-health-yoshihide-suga-726ac43cceb4b94fe2b532bdea704410.

36 Kosuke Takeuchi, "All Abe's men: Japan's economy ministry sidelined under Suga," *Nikkei Asia* (September 17, 2020), https://asia.nikkei.com/Politics/Japan-after-Abe/All-Abe-s-men-Japan-s-economy-ministry-sidelined-under-Suga.

37 Valerie Volcovici, "China calls for global 'green revolution' as Trump goes solo on climate," *Reuters* (September 23, 2020), https://www.reuters.com/article/us-un-assembly-climatechange-idINKCN26D2DH.z

38 Yuki Fujita, "Japan's new leader wants Suganomics to take off immediately," *Nikkei Asia* (September 18, 2020), https://asia.nikkei.com/Politics/Japan-after-Abe/Japan-s-new-leader-wants-Suganomics-to-take-off-immediately.

39 Nikkei, "Suga vows to meet Japan's zero-emissions goal by 2050," *Nikkei Asia* (October 26, 2020), https://asia.nikkei.com/Politics/Suga-vows-to-meet-Japan-s-zero-emissions-goal-by-2050.

40 Nikkei, "Japan creates $19bn green fund to push hydrogen planes and carbon recycling," *Nikkei Asia* (December 4, 2020), https://asia.nikkei.com/Spotlight/Environment/Climate-Change/Japan-creates-19bn-green-fund-to-push-hydrogen-planes-and-carbon-recycling.

41 Yukio Tajima and Takuya Mizorogi, "Suga Embarks on 'Green' Diplomacy, Starting With US Climate Summit," *Nikkei Asia* (December 10, 2020), https://asia.nikkei.com/Spotlight/Environment/Climate-Change/Suga-embarks-on-green-diplomacy-starting-with-US-climate-summit.

42  Nikkei, "Japan strives to lessen LNG supply chain's environmental burden," *Nikkei Asia* (October 10, 2020), https://asia.nikkei.com/Business/Energy/Japan-strives-to-lessen-LNG-supply-chain-s-environmental-burden; Llewelyn Hughes, "Now is the time for Australia and Japan to work together on a low-carbon future," *East Asia Forum* (November 28, 2020), https://www.eastasiaforum.org/2020/11/28/now-is-the-time-for-australia-and-japan-to-work-together-on-a-low-carbon-future/.

43  Satoshi Kurokawa, "Can the US–Japan Climate Partnership lead decarbonisation in Asia?" *East Asia Forum* (June 2, 2021).

44  "Japan to shut or mothball 100 ageing coal-fired power plants -Yomiuri," *Reuters* (July 2, 2020), https://www.reuters.com/article/uk-japan-powerstation-coal-idUKKBN24306U.

45  "Toshiba stops taking orders for coal-fired power plants," *Nikkei Asia* (November 10, 2020), https://asia.nikkei.com/Spotlight/Environment/Toshiba-stops-taking-orders-for-coal-fired-power-plants.

46  Jun Arima, "Reclaiming pragmatism in Japan's energy policy," *East Asia Forum* (April 3, 2021), https://www.eastasiaforum.org/2021/04/03/reclaiming-pragmatism-in-japans-energy-policy/.

47  Robin Harding, "Japan PM Suga's net-zero pledge sparks fierce debate," *Financial Times* (July 23, 2021), https://www.ft.com/content/6e07b43b-b4a7-45b0-9005-021bb9e6ff4f.

48  Takaki Tominaga, "FOCUS: Japan looks to renewables, role of nuclear elusive ahead of election," *Kyodo News* (October 29, 2021), https://english.kyodonews.net/news/2021/10/604995b5eef2-focus-japan-looks-to-renewables-role-of-nuclear-elusive-ahead-of-election.html.

49  Shunsuke Shigeta, Kosuke Takeuchi and Junichi Sugihara, "Japan tilts toward nuclear energy with METI back in driver's seat," *Nikkei Asia* (October 8, 2021), https://asia.nikkei.com/Politics/Japan-tilts-toward-nuclear-energy-with-METI-back-in-driver-s-seat.

50  "Nuclear hawks under Kishida threaten Suga's renewables push," *The Asahi Shimbun* (October 14, 2021), https://www.asahi.com/ajw/articles/14460623; Nikkei, "Nuclear power crucial to Japan's net-zero goal: industry minister," *Nikkei Asia* (October 6, 2021), https://asia.nikkei.com/Business/Energy/Nuclear-power-crucial-to-Japan-s-net-zero-goal-industry-minister

51  Junichiro Nagasaki, Satoshi Shinden, Masatoshi Toda and Shinichi Sekine, "Japan's clean energy strategy to push nuclear technologies," *The Asahi Shimbun* (January 19, 2022), https://www.asahi.com/ajw/articles/14525409.

52  "Japan PM vows to push for green, digital transformation," *The Mainichi* (January 19, 2022), https://mainichi.jp/english/articles/20220119/p2g/00m/0na/025000c.

53   Shunsuke Shigeta, Kosuke Takeuchi, and Junichi Sugihara, "Japan tilts toward nuclear energy with METI back in driver's seat," *Nikkei Asia* (October 8, 2021), https://asia.nikkei.com/Politics/Japan-tilts-toward-nuclear-energy-with-METI-back-in-driver-s-seat#.

54   "Japan nuclear research set to revive on U.S. fast-reactor project," *Nikkei Asia* (January 3, 2022), https://asia.nikkei.com/Business/Energy/Japan-nuclear-research-set-to-revive-on-U.S.-fast-reactor-project.

55   "Hooked on coal for power, Japan aims for ammonia fix," *The Asahi Shimbun* (November 1, 2021), https://www.asahi.com/ajw/articles/14472880.

56   Juntaro Arai, "Japan's ammonia push in Southeast Asia seen as aiding coal," *Nikkei Asia*, https://asia.nikkei.com/Spotlight/Environment/Climate-Change/Japan-s-ammonia-push-in-Southeast-Asia-seen-as-aiding-coal.

57   Walter Sim, "Japan should invest more in renewables and less in 'clean coal': Climate think-tank," Strait Times (February 14, 2022), https://www.straitstimes.com/asia/east-asia/japan-should-invest-more-in-renewables-and-less-in-clean-coal-climate-think-tank.

58   Mitsuru Obe, "Climate for change? Japan's net zero goal tests PM Kishida's will," *Nikkei Asia* (October 12, 2021).

59   Kochi Hasegawa, "A Crisis of Democracy: Civil Society and Energy Politics Before and After the Fukushima Nuclear Disaster," in *Crisis Narratives, Institutional Change, and the Transformation of the Japanese State*, ed. Sebastian Maslow and Christian Wirth (Albany: State University of New York Press, 2021): 109–133.

60   For survey data, see Cabinet Office, https://survey.gov-online.go.jp/h28/h28-ondanka/index.html.

61   Florentine Koppenborg and Ulv Hanssen, "Japan's Climate Change Discourse: Toward Climate Securitisation?" *Politics and Governance* 9, no. 4 (2021): 53-64. For a general discussion on the security-climate change nexus, see Matt McDonald, "Climate change and security: towards ecological security?" *International Theory* 10, no. 2 (2018): 153-180.

62   Jun Nagashima, "Can the Quad Lay the Groundwork for Environmental and Economic Security? Eliminating Vulnerabilities and Ensuring Resilience," Sasakawa Peace Foundation (October 28, 2021), https://www.spf.org/iina/en/articles/nagashima_09.html.

63   "Quad ministers address Indo-Pacific 'coercion,' climate, COVID," *The Japan News* (February 11, 2022), https://the-japan-news.com/news/article/0008266212.

## Part 1.  The Border Wall on the Korean Peninsula in Global Context

_____ Reece Jones

Alatout, Samer. 2009. Walls as technologies of government: The double construction of geographies of peace and conflict in Israeli politics, 2002–present. _Annals of the Association of American Geographers_, 99, no. 5: 956–968.

Amilhat-Szary, Anne Laure and Giraut, Frédéric (eds) 2015. _Borderities and the Politics of Contemporary Mobile Borders_. Basingstoke: Palgrave Macmillan.

Andersson, Ruben. 2014. _Illegality, Inc.: Clandestine Migration and the Business of Bordering Europe_. Berkeley: University of California Press.

Belcher, Oliver, Martin, Lauren, and Tazzioli, Martina. 2015. Editorial – border struggles: epistemologies, ontologies and politics. _darkmatter_ 12, October 5.

Blomley, Nick. 2003. Law, property and the geography of violence: The frontier, the survey and the grid. _Annals of the Association of American Geographers_ 93: 121–4.

Bissonnette, Andreanne. and Vallet, Elisabet. 2020. _Border and Border Walls: In-Security, Symbolism, Vulnerabilities_. London: Routledge.

Brambilla, Chiara. 2015. Exploring the critical potential of the borderscapes concept. _Geopolitics_ 20(1): 14 – 34.

Brown, Wendy. 2014. _Walled States, Waning Sovereignty_. New York: Zone Books.

Burridge. Andrew. Gill, Nick. Kocher, Austin. and Martin, Lauren. 2017. Editorial – Polymorphic borders. _Territory, Politics, Governance_ 5(3): 239 – 251.

Cohen, Shaul. 2006. Israel's West Bank barrier: An impediment to peace? _Geographical Review_ 96(4): 682–695.

Cons, Jason, and Sanyal, Romola. 2013. Geographies at the margin: Borders in South Asia—An introduction. *Political Geography* 35: 5–13.

De León, Jason. 2015. *The Land of Open Graves: Living and Dying on the Migrant Trail.* Oakland: University of California Press.

Dear, Michael 2013. *Why Walls Won't Work: Repairing the US-Mexico Divide.* Oakland: University of California Press.

Di Cintio, Marcello. 2012. *Walls: Travels along the Barricades.* Goose Lane Editions.

Doucette, Jamie and Lee, Seung−Ook. 2015. Experimental territoriality: Assembling the Kaesong Industrial Complex in North Korea. *Political Geography.* 47: 53–63.

Elden, Stuart. 2010. Land, terrain, territory. *Progress in Human Geography.* 26(6): 799–817.

Elden, Stuart. 2013. *The Birth of Territory.* Chicago: University of Chicago Press.

Ferdoush, Azmeary. 2018. Seeing borders through the lens of structuration: A theoretical framework. *Geopolitics* 23(1): 180–200.

Harvey, P.D.A. 1993. *Maps in Tudor England,* Chicago: University of Chicago Press.

Harley, J.B. 2002. *The New Nature of Maps,* P. Laxton, ed., Baltimore: Johns Hopkins Press.

Harley, J.B and Woodward, David. 1987. *The History of Cartography,* vol. 1, Chicago: University of Chicago Press.

Herskovitz, John. 2009. North Korea New Year wish: tear down imaginary wall. *Reuters,* December 29.

Johnson, Corey, Jones, Reece, Paasi, Anssi, Amoore, Louise, Mountz, Alison, Salter, Mark, and Rumford, Chris. 2011. Interventions on rethinking 'the border' in border studies. *Political Geography* 30(2): 61 – 69.

Jones, Reece. 2012. *Border Walls: Security and the War on Terror in the United States, India, and Israel.* London: Zed Books.

Jones, Reece. 2012. Spaces of refusal: rethinking sovereign power and resistance at the border. *Annals of the Association of American Geographers* 102(3): 685 – 699.

Jones, Reece 2016. *Violent Borders: Refugees and the Right to Move*. London: Verso.

Jones, Reece and Johnson, Corey. (eds) 2014. *Placing the Border in the Everyday Life*. Farnham – Burlington: Ashgate.

Jones, Reece, Johnson, Corey, Brown, Wendy, Popescu, Gabriel, Pallister-Wilkins, Polly, Mountz, Alison, and Gilbert, Emily. 2017. Interventions on the State of Sovereignty at the Border *Political Geography*. 59: 1-10.

Kim, Chong Yun. 2021. Tunnel discovery at the DMZ, a monumental achievement by the Far East District. *Defense Visual Information Distribution Service*, July 15.

Kuhn, Anthony. 2019. Hundreds of thousands of landmines remain from Korean War but serve no purpose. *National Public Radio*, August 27.

Lee, Kyungsoo and Lee, Seung-Ook. 2021. Unravelling local dynamics in the Sino-North Korean border region *Geopolitics*, https://doi.org/10.1080/14650045.2021.1992388.

Lee, Steven. 2013. The Korean Armistice and the end of peace: The US-UN coalition and the dynamics of war-making in Korea, 1953 – 76. *Journal of Korean Studies* 18 (2): 183 – 224.

Longo, Matthew. 2017. *The Politics of Borders: Sovereignty, Security, and the Citizen after 9/11*. Cambridge: Cambridge University Press.

Lovell, Julia. 2006. *The Great Wall: China Against the World*. New York: Grove Press.

Miller, Todd. 2017. *Storming the Wall: Climate Change, Migration, and Homeland Security*. City Lights Press.

Nail, Thomas. 2016. *Theory of the Border*. New York: Oxford University Press.

Oberdorfer, Dan, and Carlin, Robert. 2013. *The Two Koreas: A Contemporary History*. New York: Basic Books.

Pallister-Wilkins, Polly. 2011. The separation wall: A symbol of power and a site of resistance? *Antipode* 43 (5): 1851-1882.

Park, Terry. 2019. The de/militarised frontier: the Korean demilitarised zone, the American DMZ border guard, and US liberal empire. *Critical Military Studies* 4(25): 237-254.

Parker, Noel and Vaughan-Williams, Nick. 2009. Lines in the sand: towards an agenda for critical border studies. *Geopolitics* 14(3): 582 – 587.

Parker, Noel. and Vaughan-Williams, Nick. 2012. Critical border studies: broadening and deepening the 'lines in the sand' agenda. *Geopolitics* 17(4): 727 – 733.

Phillips, Kristine. 2019. As Trump pushes for a wall, authorities keep finding drug tunnels under the U.S.-Mexico border. *The Washington Post*, January 15.

Rael, Ronald. 2017. *Borderwall as Architecture: A Manifesto for the U.S.-Mexico Boundary*. Oakland: University of California Press.

Rosière, Stéphane and Jones, Reece. 2012. Teichopolitics: Re-considering globalisation through the role of walls and fences. *Geopolitics*, 17(1): 217-234.

Sack, Robert. 1986. *Human Territoriality: Its Theory and History*. Cambridge: Cambridge University Press.

Sahlins, Peter. 1991. *Boundaries: The Making of France and Spain in the Pyrenees*. Oakland: University of California Press.

Scott, James C. 2009. *The Art of Not Being Governed: An Anarchist History of Upland Southeast Asia*. New Haven: Yale University Press.

Scott, James C. 2017. *Against the Grain: A Deep History of the Earliest States*. New Haven: Yale University Press.

Slack, Jeremy, Martinez, Daniel, and Whiteford, Scott. 2018. *The Shadow of the Wall: Violence and Migration on The U.S.-Mexico Border*. Tucson: University of Arizona Press.

Till, Karen, Sundberg, Juanita, Pullan, Wendy, Psaltis, Charis, Makriyianni, Chara, Celal, Rana, Samani, Meltem, and Dowler, Lorraine. 2012. Interventions in the political geographies of walls. *Political Geography* 33: 52-62.

Vallet, Elisabeth. and David, Charles-Phillip. 2012. The rebuilding of the wall in International Relations. *Journal of Borderlands Studies.* 27(2): 111-119.

Vallet, Elisabeth. Editor. 2014. *Borders, Fences and Walls: State of Insecurity?* London: Ashgate.

Walia, Harsha. 2013. *Undoing Border Imperialism.* Oakland: AK Press.

Walia, Harsha. 2021. *Border and Rule: Global Migration, Capitalism, and the Rise of Racist Nationalism.* New York: Haymarket Books.

Walker, RBJ 1993. *Inside/Outside: International Relations as Political Theory.* Cambridge: Cambridge University Press.

Walters, William. 2015. Reflections on migration and governmentality. *Movements: Journal für kritische Migrations - und Grenzregimeforschung* 1(1): 1 - 25.

Wilson, Thomas. and Donnan, Hastings. (eds) 2012. *A Companion to Border Studies.* Chichester: Blackwell Publishing.

Winichakul, Thongchai. 1994. *Siam Mapped: A History of the Geo-Body of a Nation.* Honolulu: University of Hawai'i Press.

## Part 2. China's Low-Carbon Economy: Trends and Outlook _____ Wang, Hongxia

Guan, D., Shan, Y., Zheng, H. *et al.* 2018. China $CO_2$ emission accounts 1997 - 2015. *Scientific Data* 5, 170201. https://doi.org/10.1038/sdata.2017.201

Liu, Jianggang. 2012. *An Empirical Study of Carbon Dioxide Emissions Based on the Perspective of Energy Utilization.* Unpublished Doctoral Dissertation. Shanghai Academy of Social Sciences, Shanghai.

An Empirical Study of Carbon Dioxide Emissions Based on the Perspective of Energy Utilization 基于能源利用视角的二氧化碳排放实证研究

Wang, Feng. Wu, Lihua. Yang, Chao. 2010. Driving Factors for Growth of Carbon

Dioxide Emissions During Economic Development in China, *Economic Research Journal(Chinese)*, 45(2): 123-136.

http://www.erj.cn/cn/gwqk2.aspx?m=20100918141426890803

The State Council Information Office of the People's Republic of China. 2021. *Responding to Climate Change: China's Policies and Actions*. The State Council Information Office of the People's Republic of China.

http://www.scio.gov.cn/zfbps/32832/Document/1715506/1715506.htm

National Bureau of Statistics of China. 2021. *Statistical Communiqué of the People's Republic of China on the 2020 National Economic and Social Development*. National Bureau of Statistics of China.

http://www.stats.gov.cn/english/PressRelease/202102/t20210228_1814177.html

The State Council of China: Guiding Opinions of the State Council on Accelerating the Establishment and Improvement of a Green and Low-Carbon Circular Development Economic System. 中国国务院: 国务院关于加快建立健全绿色低碳循环发展经济体系的指导意见。

http://www.gov.cn/zhengce/content/2021-02/22/content_5588274.htm.

bp. 2021. Statistical Review of World Energy 2021. https://www.bp.com/en/global/corporate/energy-economics/statistical-review-of-world-energy.html

Department of Energy Statistics. 2021. *China Energy Statistical Yearbook 2020*. China Statistics Press.

National Bureau of Statistics of China. 2020. China Statistical Yearbook 2020.

http://www.stats.gov.cn/tjsj/ndsj/

## Part 7. North Korea's Climate Change and Implications for Inter-Korean Cooperation _____ Myeong, Soojeong

DPRK. 2016. *Intended Nationally Determined Contribution of Democratic People's Repub-*

*lic of Korea.*

DPRK. 2019. *Updated nationally determined contribution of the DPRK.*

DPRK, UNEP. 2012. *Democratic People's Republic of Korea environmental and climate change outlook.*

Heo, et al. 2018. Future sea level projections over the seas around Korea from CMIP5 simulations. *Atmosphere. Korean Meteorological Society.* Vol. 28, No. 1 (2018) pp. 25-35.

KMA. 2012. *Climate change projection of Korean Peninsula Report.* Korea Meteorological Administration.

Myeong et al. 2021. *North Korea's vulnerability to climate change and inter-Korean cooperation to respond to climate change (I).* Korea Environment Institute.

Myeong et al. 2013. *A study on constricting a cooperative system for South and North Koreas to counteract climate change on the Korean Peninsula III.* Korea Environment Institute.

NIMS. 2020. *Climate change projection of Korean Peninsula Report - Climate change projection based on SSP-2.6/SSP5-8.5.* National Institute of Meteorological Sciences.

NIMS. 2018. 100 *Years of climate change on the Korean Peninsula.* National Institute of Meteorological Sciences.

## Part 8. Cooperation between South and North Koreas for net-zero emissions on the Korean Peninsula with NBS & REDD+ _____ Jang, Won Seok

Baquedano, F. G., Zereyesus, Y. A., Valdes, C., & Ajewole, K. 2021. *International Food Security Assessment 2021-31.* No. 1962-2021-2203.

Berenguer et al. 2021. "Chapter 19 : Drivers and ecological Impacts of deforestation and forest degradation." *Science Panel for the Amazon(SPA)* 2021(16), pp. 12-21.

Cheung, W. W., Reygondeau, G., & Frölicher, T. L. 2016. "Large benefits to marine fisheries of meeting the 1.5 C global warming target." *Science*. 354(6319), pp. 1591-1594.

Cohen-Shacham, E., Walters, G., Janzen, C., & Maginnis, S. 2016. *Nature-based solutions to address global societal challenges*. IUCN: Gland, Switzerland, 97.

Corbera, E., & Schroeder, H. 2011. "Governing and implementing REDD+." *Environmental science & policy*. 14(2), pp. 89-99.

Faivre, N., Fritz, M., Freitas, T., de Boissezon, B., & Vandewoestijne, S. 2017. "Nature-Based Solutions in the EU: Innovating with nature to address social, economic and environmental challenges." *Environmental research*. 159, pp. 509-518.

Finlayson, C. 2018. "World Wide Fund for Nature (WWF)." In *The wetland book I: Structure and function, management and methods*. pp. 727-731. Springer.

IPCC AR6. 2021. *Intergovernmental Panel on Climate Change (IPCC) report AR6*.

Janzen, R., Davis, M., & Kumar, A. 2020. "Evaluating long-term greenhouse gas mitigation opportunities through carbon capture, utilization, and storage in the oil sands." *Energy*. 209, 118364.

Jiang, K., Ashworth, P., Zhang, S., Liang, X., Sun, Y., & Angus, D. 2020. "China's carbon capture, utilization and storage (CCUS) policy: A critical review." *Renewable and Sustainable Energy Reviews*, 119, 109601.

Kabisch, N., Frantzeskaki, N., Pauleit, S., Naumann, S., Davis, M., Artmann, M., ... & Bonn, A. 2016. "Nature-based solutions to climate change mitigation and adaptation in urban areas: perspectives on indicators, knowledge gaps, barriers, and opportunities for action." *Ecology and Societ*. 21(2).

Kulessa, M. 2010. "UNIDO–United Nations Industrial Development Organization." In *A Concise Encyclopedia of the United Nations*. pp. 732-732. Brill Nijhoff.

Lee, Seung-Wook et al. 2017. "Recent Trends of Meteorological Research in North

Korea (2007-2016): Focusing on Journal of Weather and Hydrology." *Atmosphere.* 27 (4), pp. 411-422.

Leonzio, G., Foscolo, P. U., Zondervan, E., & Bogle, I. D. L. 2020. "Scenario analysis of carbon capture, utilization (particularly producing methane and methanol), and storage (CCUS) systems." *Industrial & Engineering Chemistry Research.* 59(15), pp. 6961-6976.

Li, N., Pacheco-Fabig, M., & Steed, M. 2018. *International Union for Conservation of Nature (IUCN). Yearbook of International Environmental Law.* 29, pp. 476-492.

Minasny, Budiman, et al. 2017. "Soil carbon 4 per mille." *Geoderma.* 292, pp. 59-86.

Moghaddasi, H., Culp, C., Vanegas, J., & Ehsani, M. 2021. "Net Zero Energy Buildings: Variations, Clarifications, and Requirements in Response to the Paris Agreement." *Energies.* 14(13),

Oh, Seung Min et al. 2017. "Estimating of the Greenhouse Gas Mitigation and Function of Water Resources Conservation through Conservation of Surface Soils Erosion and Policy Suggestion," *Journal of Soil Groundwater Environ.* 22 (6), pp. 74-84. (in Korean)

Park, Kyung Seok. 2013. "North Korea's Forests: Current Situation and Policy," *Korea Rural Economic Institute Quarterly Agricultural Trends in North Korea* 15 (3), pp. 3-23.

Rogelj, J., Luderer, G., Pietzcker, R. C., Kriegler, E., Schaeffer, M., Krey, V., & Riahi, K. 2015. "Energy system transformations for limiting end-of-century warming to below 1.5 C." *Nature Climate Change.* 5(6), pp. 519-527.

Rogelj, J., Schaeffer, M., Meinshausen, M., Knutti, R., Alcamo, J., Riahi, K., & Hare, W. 2015. "Zero emission targets as long-term global goals for climate protection." *Environmental Research Letters.* 10(10), 105007.

Seok, Hyundeok et al. 2014. *The Strategy of Restoration and Conservation of Deforested and Degraded Mountainous Areas in North Korea.* Korea Rural Economic Institute

(in Korean)

Su, Xuanming, et al. 2017. "Emission pathways to achieve 2.0° C and 1.5° C climate targets." *Earth's Future*. 5.6. pp. 592-604.

Tanaka, K., & O'Neill, B. C. 2018. "The Paris Agreement zero-emissions goal is not always consistent with the 1.5°C and 2°C temperature targets." Nature Climate Change. 8(4), pp. 319-324.

UN-REDD programme, "ABOUT REDD+." https://www.unredd.net/about/what-is-redd-plus.html.

van de Ven, D. J., Westphal, M., González-Eguino, M., Gambhir, A., Peters, G., Sognnaes, I., & Clarke, L. 2021. "The Impact of US Re-engagement in Climate on the Paris Targets." *Earth's Future*. 9(9), e2021EF002077.

van Soest, H. L., den Elzen, M. G., & van Vuuren, D. P. 2021. "Net-zero emission targets for major emitting countries consistent with the Paris Agreement." *Nature communications*. 12(1), pp. 1-9.

WFP and FAO. 2021. "Hunger Hotspots. FAO-WFP early warnings on acute food insecurity: August to November 2021 outlook". FAO

Supra-National Cooperation and Communication
for Reaching Carbon Neutrality

# Border and Environment

초판인쇄  2022년 4월 29일
초판발행  2022년 4월 29일

지은이  HK + National Strategies Research Project Agency,
　　　　Center for International Area Studies,
　　　　Hankuk University of Foreign Studies
펴낸이  채종준(Jong-Jun Chae)
펴낸곳  한국학술정보(주)(Korean Studies Information Co., Ltd.)
주　소  경기도 파주시 회동길 230(문발동)(230, Hoedong-gil, Paju-si, Gyeonggi-do, Korea)
전　화  031-908-3181(대표)
팩　스  031-908-3189
홈페이지  http://ebook.kstudy.com
E-mail  출판사업부 publish@kstudy.com
출판신고  2003년 9월 25일 제406-2003-000012호

ISBN    979-11-6801-448-0 93340